A Family Journey
through Doctrine

A Family Journey through Doctrine

A 60-Day Family Worship Guide

JUSTIN MILLER

RESOURCE *Publications* · Eugene, Oregon

A FAMILY JOURNEY THROUGH DOCTRINE
A 60-Day Family Worship Guide

Resource Publications
An Imprint of Wipf and Stock Publishers
199 W. 8th Ave., Suite 3
Eugene, OR 97401

www.wipfandstock.com

PAPERBACK ISBN: 978-1-7252-6817-3
HARDCOVER ISBN: 978-1-7252-6809-8
EBOOK ISBN: 978-1-7252-6816-6

05/14/21

To the Triune God who saved this unholy sinner by immeasurable love and grace in Christ's person, life, and work alone. My aim in life is to give you praise and glory in all I do. You are what this redeemed sinner wants above all else. My highest delight and greatest desire are to live in your presence where joy abounds forevermore.

To my wife and kids. I pray the truths presented here permeate our hearts and minds bringing forth faith by God's sovereign grace as well as transforming us into the image of Christ to the praise of God's grace.

Contents

Introduction: Why does this matter?

"Why does this matter?!" As a parent, I have heard my kids ask the question on more than one occasion, "Why does this matter?" What they are seeking and desiring to grasp is the importance of what they are learning. For example, my children do not often see the importance of learning multiplication because they lack the necessary understanding of its importance for their future lives. They will need to know multiplication as they handle their own finances, as they shop, even as they do basic calculations with regards to recipes or even taking medicine. Learning to multiply is an important skill to acquire. Oftentimes in the moment we lack the perspective of what is best for us before God. Christians make the same mistake when asking the question of family devotion time "why does this matter?" Often, we do not see the Scriptures read, discussed, memorized, understood, and sung for what it is. It is a means of grace that God gives to bring our children to faith in Christ, to grow our families in the knowledge of Christ as well as in our loving devotion to His glory. Every man, particularly, is a pastor of his own family. As Christians we are called to lead our family to know God and enjoy Him. Therefore, to answer the question about the importance of a daily family devotion time "why does it matter?" It matters for families to know God and grow in grace. Nothing matters more each day.

One of the greatest areas of resistance in this arena of learning truth as families is an anti-doctrine mindset. In our modern context I have heard many demean the importance of learning Christian doctrine by saying, "it is not practical" or "it does not affect me when I climb up into the combine or sit in my cubicle." However, Christian doctrine does matter when you climb up into the combine or sit in your cubicle. Christian doctrine will shape your entire worldview and will even forge your own self-view. It grounds your understanding of life and all therein with the Creator's perspective. It will change how you work in your combine or cubicle, likely without you discerning its impact until a portion of time has passed. It will affect how you view your life, family, and job. It will alter how you spend time and money. It will shape and form you. The truth of the Christian faith is the means God has decreed to use to transform His people into His Son's image. Is it any wonder that Paul wrote in Romans 12:2, "2 Do not be conformed to this world, *but be transformed by the renewal of your mind*, that by testing you may discern what is the will of God, what is good and acceptable and perfect." Paul tells the Roman Christians to be transformed in their everyday lives by the "renewal" of their minds. We know that Scripture per 2 Timothy 3:16–17 is the means by which God has ordained to renew our minds, bring us to maturity in thought and life, and equip us for every good work. Therefore, understanding the beliefs of the Christian faith derived from Holy Scripture is imperative for us in our everyday life. Truth is imperative for everyday life. It matters eternally, even if in a moment of time we cannot understand how doctrines like the hypostatic union (the two distinct natures of Christ, full deity and full sinless humanity, united in the one person of Jesus of Nazareth) matter for us to know in our present time. That truth teaches us something about our Savior and shapes our view of Him which alters our affections and guides our wills. Truth transforms all those whom God loves.

The aim of this book is to equip couples and families to grow in the truths of the Scriptures together. To understand in a greater way the faith once and for all delivered to God's beloved people. To take a family journey through doctrine.

Acknowledgement

Will and Brandon. Thank you for your help with this project. It is an honor to call you both friends and co-laborers in the Gospel.

Family Worship Overview and Instructions

[18] "You shall therefore lay up these words of mine in your heart and in your soul, and you shall bind them as a sign on your hand, and they shall be as frontlets between your eyes. [19] *You shall teach them to your children, talking of them when you are sitting in your house, and when you are walking by the way, and when you lie down, and when you rise.* [20] You shall write them on the doorposts of your house and on your gates, [21] that your days and the days of your children may be multiplied in the land that the Lord swore to your fathers to give them, as long as the heavens are above the earth.[1]
Deuteronomy 11:18–21

METHODOLOGY OF FAMILY WORSHIP

What a privilege it is for God's people to have the complete canon of Holy Scripture. In Deuteronomy 11:18–21 we observe the intention of God even in the opening Pentateuch of the Bible; for His redeemed people to grow in their knowledge and love for Him by discussing the Word in the family setting. Faithfulness as a family to discuss the Scripture daily was connected in Deuteronomy 11:21 to the outcome of the family enjoying the promises of God given in the Mosaic covenant. God's precepts, commands, and promises

---

1. All Scripture References are ESV unless otherwise noted.

are a blessing to His purchased people in Christ. This book aims at making family worship a systematic yet joyful time of learning from God's Word for families. A time to grow in knowledge of the Word of God and love for the God who has revealed Himself to us in His Word.

In order to make *A Family Journey through Doctrine* as clear as possible there are a few simple instructions and steps to be outlined before we jump into Day 1. Every day as a family (all Biblically married couples are a family unit, including couples with no children) there are 6 things you will do in a span of approximately 20 minutes.

THE 6 DAILY FAMILY WORSHIP STEPS

1. Read the Scripture (5 minutes)
2. Discuss the Scripture (5 minutes)
3. Memorize the Scripture (2 Minutes)
4. Doctrines of Scripture (2 Minutes)
5. Sing Scriptural Truth (3 Minutes)
6. Pray the Truth (3 Minutes)

READ THE SCRIPTURE (5 MINUTES)

Prayerfully pick a book of the Bible on Day 1 and commit, as a family, to read a few verses at a time through that book of the Bible each day. Do not feel like you must read large chunks, especially if you have young kids. It is also helpful to pray before you begin reading the Scripture, specifically to ask God, who is the giver of all good things, for understanding of what you as a family are about to read. He is the divine author of Scripture and He leads His people in truth from His Word.

DISCUSS THE SCRIPTURE (5 MINUTES)

Upon reading the Scripture passage for the day, take five minutes to ask four questions as a family in order to study the Scripture rightly together. *(For help in understanding the text and answering these questions there are great study Bibles like the ESV Study Bible or Reformation Study Bible that would be tremendously helpful)*

Ask Four Questions:

1. Who wrote this Biblical book; to whom is it written; and what is the book's main theme?—*If you are in a book of the Bible for a long time* (Ex. Going verse by verse through Romans) *still ask this question as it reminds everyone how to approach the examination of the Scriptural passage you are reading,* namely to understand the passage in light of the main point of the book you are going through.
2. What is the author's point in this Scriptural passage?
3. What does this Scriptural passage teach us about God, man, salvation, and life?
4. How do I apply the truth in this Scriptural passage to my life?

MEMORIZE THE SCRIPTURE (2 MINUTES)

One member of the family should *read the selected Scripture* out loud *three times* with the family in order to memorize.

On the second and third time reading the Scripture out loud, *have all the family repeat the Scripture after the person reads* the passage.

Every 10 days each member of the family should be asked to recite the Scripture by memory. If they are still struggling to memorize the Scripture, that is fine, just keeping work through it. The next day presents a new Scripture to memorize with the above formula. Continue with previously memorized Scripture by having a family member or two recite it from memory each day to keep it fresh in the mind.

DOCTRINES OF SCRIPTURE (2 MINUTES)

Each day has a catechism (a theological question and answer) to learn doctrine.

Read the question out loud and then read the answer out loud. *Do this three times and on the third repetition ask the question again and then have them answer on their own.*

Question and Answer formats (Catechisms) have historically been the way the church has taught doctrine in family settings.

SING SCRIPTURAL TRUTH (3 MINUTES)

Each day will have a song to sing. While that may seem intimidating, especially if you are not musical like I am. However, singing together is essential because when you sing the same song for several days of the program, the family will all learn the lyrics of rich theological hymns and even how to sing them. To get started it would be helpful to simply look up the hymn for the day on YouTube and sing along with it from the phone or computer. What you will find is the lyrics and melody become embedded in your minds and its truths permeate your thoughts over time. Singing in Scripture has always been part of the worship of God in both the Old and New Testaments (Psalms, Psalm 95:2, Acts 16:25, Ephesians 5:19, Colossians 3:16).

PRAY THE TRUTH (3 MINUTES)

Each session ends by praying the truth.

Begin the prayer by *praising God* for a characteristic you have studied about Him, *petition (ask) him,* in Christ, to forgive sin and meet various needs you want to bring before Him (especially the salvation of your children), and then *thank Him for His grace* in salvation and various areas of your family's life. This follows the ideology of the Lord's Prayer (Matthew 6:9–10) as well as heeds Paul's admonition to give thanks in all things (1 Thessalonians 5:18).

The formula for family prayer is:

1. **Praise** (Highlighting God's attributes and giving Him praise and glory)
2. **Petition** (Asking God, in Christ, to forgive sin and meet needs per His will and for His glory)
3. **Thank** (Thanking God for His grace and praising Him)

WHAT ABOUT WHEN I HAVE FINISHED THE PROGRAM?—REPEAT FROM DAY 1 WITH MODIFICATIONS.

After you have finished the 60-day program, you simply start again on Day 1 with where you are at in the book of the Bible you are reading through.

Over time, you will want to substitute other Scriptures for memorization, other hymns to learn and sing, and other doctrinal question and answer sets to go over (such as the *Westminster Shorter Catechism* or the *New City Catechism*).

In addition, in the *Doctrines of Scripture* section you may, for a season, choose to memorize church creeds (Apostles, Nicene, Athanasian) by reading the Creed sentence by sentence, having each member of the family repeat each sentence after the reader (see appendix 8 for three church Creeds to memorize in order to grow in understanding of doctrine).

Day 1

READ THE SCRIPTURE (5 MINUTES)

Pray for God to grant understanding of the passage of Scripture then read out loud the passage of Scripture in the book of the Bible you are going through verse-by-verse as a family.

DISCUSS THE SCRIPTURE (5 MINUTES)

Four Questions:

1. Who wrote this Biblical book; to whom was it written; and what is the book's main theme? *Always ask this question as it reminds everyone how to approach the examination of the Scriptural passage (in light of books overall theme) you are reading.*
2. What is the author's point in this Scriptural passage?
3. What does this Scriptural passage teach us about God, man, salvation, and life?
4. How do I apply the truth in this Scriptural passage to my life?

MEMORIZE THE SCRIPTURE (2 MINUTES)

Genesis 1:1
1 In the beginning, God created the heavens and the earth.

DOCTRINES OF SCRIPTURE (2 MINUTES)

What is the Bible?

The Bible is the inspired, authoritative Word of God.
(2 Timothy 3:16–17)

The Bible, in its original autographs, is without error in all that it teaches. *(Old Testament—Hebrew and little Aramaic, New Testament—Greek)*

SING SCRIPTURAL TRUTH (3 MINUTES)

Amazing Grace (Lyrics in Appendix 1)

PRAY THE TRUTH (3 MINUTES)

- *Praise*
- *Petition*
- *Thank*

Day 2

READ THE SCRIPTURE (5 MINUTES)

Pray for God to grant understanding of the passage of Scripture then read out loud the passage of Scripture in the book of the Bible you are going through verse-by-verse as a family.

DISCUSS THE SCRIPTURE (5 MINUTES)

Four Questions:

1. Who wrote this Biblical book, to whom was it written, and what is the book's main theme? *Always ask this question as it reminds everyone how to approach the examination of the Scriptural passage (in light of books overall theme) you are reading.*
2. What is the author's point in this Scriptural passage?
3. What does this Scriptural passage teach us about God, man, salvation, and life?
4. How do I apply the truth in this Scriptural passage to my life?

MEMORIZE THE SCRIPTURE (2 MINUTES)

Genesis 1:1
1 In the beginning, God created the heavens and the earth.

Day 2

DOCTRINES OF SCRIPTURE (2 MINUTES)

What is a Biblical Covenant?

A Biblical covenant is an agreement between God and man. Or an agreement within the Triune God Himself *(Covenant of Redemption)*.

There are seven covenants recorded in Holy Scripture. See Appendix 7 for descriptions of the covenants.

(Genesis—Revelation)

SING SCRIPTURAL TRUTH (3 MINUTES)

Amazing Grace (Lyrics in Appendix 1)

PRAY THE TRUTH (3 MINUTES)

- *Praise*
- *Petition*
- *Thank*

Day 3

READ THE SCRIPTURE (5 MINUTES)

Pray for God to grant understanding of the passage of Scripture then read out loud the passage of Scripture in the book of the Bible you are going through verse-by-verse as a family.

DISCUSS THE SCRIPTURE (5 MINUTES)

Four Questions:

1. Who wrote this Biblical book, to whom was it written, and what is the book's main theme? *Always ask this question as it reminds everyone how to approach the examination of the Scriptural passage (in light of books overall theme) you are reading.*
2. What is the author's point in this Scriptural passage?
3. What does this Scriptural passage teach us about God, man, salvation, and life?
4. How do I apply the truth in this Scriptural passage to my life?

MEMORIZE THE SCRIPTURE (2 MINUTES)

Genesis 1:1
1 In the beginning, God created the heavens and the earth.

DOCTRINES OF SCRIPTURE (2 MINUTES)

What are the covenants of the Bible?

Covenant of Redemption *(Ephesians 1:3–14)*, Adamic Covenant *(Genesis 2:15–17)*, Noahic Covenant *(Genesis 8:20–9:17)*, Abrahamic Covenant *(Genesis 12:1–3, Genesis 13:14–18, Genesis 15, Genesis 17)*, Mosaic Covenant *(Exodus 20—Deuteronomy 34)*, Davidic Covenant *(2 Samuel 7)*, New Covenant *(Matthew—Revelation)*.

SING SCRIPTURAL TRUTH (3 MINUTES)

Amazing Grace (Lyrics in Appendix 1)

PRAY THE TRUTH (3 MINUTES)

- *Praise*
- *Petition*
- *Thank*

Day 4

READ THE SCRIPTURE (5 MINUTES)

Pray for God to grant understanding of the passage of Scripture then read out loud the passage of Scripture in the book of the Bible you are going through verse-by-verse as a family.

DISCUSS THE SCRIPTURE (5 MINUTES)

Four Questions:

1. Who wrote this Biblical book, to whom was it written, and what is the book's main theme? *Always ask this question as it reminds everyone how to approach the examination of the Scriptural passage (in light of books overall theme) you are reading.*
2. What is the author's point in this Scriptural passage?
3. What does this Scriptural passage teach us about God, man, salvation, and life?
4. How do I apply the truth in this Scriptural passage to my life?

MEMORIZE THE SCRIPTURE (2 MINUTES)

Genesis 1:1
1 In the beginning, God created the heavens and the earth.

DOCTRINES OF SCRIPTURE (2 MINUTES)

Who is God?

God is One God, Three Eternally Distinct Persons: Father, Son, and Holy Spirit.

God is the Holy Creator and Sovereign Ruler of heaven and earth.

(John 1:1–4, Matthew 28:18–20, Genesis 1:1–2).

SING SCRIPTURAL TRUTH (3 MINUTES)

Amazing Grace (Lyrics in Appendix 1)

PRAY THE TRUTH (3 MINUTES)

- *Praise*
- *Petition*
- *Thank*

Day 5

READ THE SCRIPTURE (5 MINUTES)

Pray for God to grant understanding of the passage of Scripture then read out loud the passage of Scripture in the book of the Bible you are going through verse-by-verse as a family.

DISCUSS THE SCRIPTURE (5 MINUTES)

Four Questions:

1. Who wrote this Biblical book, to whom was it written, and what is the book's main theme? *Always ask this question as it reminds everyone how to approach the examination of the Scriptural passage (in light of books overall theme) you are reading.*
2. What is the author's point in this Scriptural passage?
3. What does this Scriptural passage teach us about God, man, salvation, and life?
4. How do I apply the truth in this Scriptural passage to my life?

MEMORIZE THE SCRIPTURE (2 MINUTES)

Genesis 1:1
1 In the beginning, God created the heavens and the earth.

DOCTRINES OF SCRIPTURE (2 MINUTES)

What are God's attributes?

God's attributes are His characteristics.

God is: Triune (One God, Three Persons), Love, Eternal, Omniscient (All Knowing), Omnipotent (All Powerful), Omnipresent (Fully everywhere at all times), Holy, Just, Righteous, Pure, Faithful, True, Merciful, and Perfect in all of His characteristics.

(Genesis—Revelation)

SING SCRIPTURAL TRUTH (3 MINUTES)

Amazing Grace (Lyrics in Appendix 1)

PRAY THE TRUTH (3 MINUTES)

- *Praise*
- *Petition*
- *Thank*

Day 6

READ THE SCRIPTURE (5 MINUTES)

Pray for God to grant understanding of the passage of Scripture then read out loud the passage of Scripture in the book of the Bible you are going through verse-by-verse as a family.

DISCUSS THE SCRIPTURE (5 MINUTES)

Four Questions:

1. Who wrote this Biblical book, to whom was it written, and what is the book's main theme? *Always ask this question as it reminds everyone how to approach the examination of the Scriptural passage (in light of books overall theme) you are reading.*
2. What is the author's point in this Scriptural passage?
3. What does this Scriptural passage teach us about God, man, salvation, and life?
4. How do I apply the truth in this Scriptural passage to my life?

MEMORIZE THE SCRIPTURE (2 MINUTES)

Genesis 1:1
1 In the beginning, God created the heavens and the earth.

DOCTRINES OF SCRIPTURE (2 MINUTES)

What is Creation?

Creation includes all of the universe and everything within it. This includes the galaxies, earth, and all of its creatures which God created and continues to sustain (Psalm 104).

SING SCRIPTURAL TRUTH (3 MINUTES)

Amazing Grace (Lyrics in Appendix 1)

PRAY THE TRUTH (3 MINUTES)

- *Praise*
- *Petition*
- *Thank*

Day 7

READ THE SCRIPTURE (5 MINUTES)

Pray for God to grant understanding of the passage of Scripture then read out loud the passage of Scripture in the book of the Bible you are going through verse-by-verse as a family.

DISCUSS THE SCRIPTURE (5 MINUTES)

Four Questions:

1. Who wrote this Biblical book, to whom was it written, and what is the book's main theme? *Always ask this question as it reminds everyone how to approach the examination of the Scriptural passage (in light of books overall theme) you are reading.*
2. What is the author's point in this Scriptural passage?
3. What does this Scriptural passage teach us about God, man, salvation, and life?
4. How do I apply the truth in this Scriptural passage to my life?

MEMORIZE THE SCRIPTURE (2 MINUTES)

Genesis 1:1
1 In the beginning, God created the heavens and the earth.

DOCTRINES OF SCRIPTURE (2 MINUTES)

What is the pinnacle of God's creation?

Man and woman is the pinnacle of God's creation as those made in the image of God (Genesis 1:26–27).

SING SCRIPTURAL TRUTH (3 MINUTES)

Amazing Grace (Lyrics in Appendix 1)

PRAY THE TRUTH (3 MINUTES)

- *Praise*
- *Petition*
- *Thank*

Day 8

READ THE SCRIPTURE (5 MINUTES)

Pray for God to grant understanding of the passage of Scripture then read out loud the passage of Scripture in the book of the Bible you are going through verse-by-verse as a family.

DISCUSS THE SCRIPTURE (5 MINUTES)

Four Questions:

1. Who wrote this Biblical book, to whom was it written, and what is the book's main theme? *Always ask this question as it reminds everyone how to approach the examination of the Scriptural passage (in light of books overall theme) you are reading.*
2. What is the author's point in this Scriptural passage?
3. What does this Scriptural passage teach us about God, man, salvation, and life?
4. How do I apply the truth in this Scriptural passage to my life?

MEMORIZE THE SCRIPTURE (2 MINUTES)

Genesis 1:1
1 In the beginning, God created the heavens and the earth.

DOCTRINES OF SCRIPTURE (2 MINUTES)

What is marriage?

God created marriage as one man and one woman in a covenant relationship as husband and wife, forsaking all others (Genesis 2:24).

Marriage is a picture of the Gospel (Ephesians 5:21–33).

SING SCRIPTURAL TRUTH (3 MINUTES)

Amazing Grace (Lyrics in Appendix 1)

PRAY THE TRUTH (3 MINUTES)

- *Praise*
- *Petition*
- *Thank*

Day 9

READ THE SCRIPTURE (5 MINUTES)

Pray for God to grant understanding of the passage of Scripture then read out loud the passage of Scripture in the book of the Bible you are going through verse-by-verse as a family.

DISCUSS THE SCRIPTURE (5 MINUTES)

Four Questions:

1. Who wrote this Biblical book, to whom was it written, and what is the book's main theme? *Always ask this question as it reminds everyone how to approach the examination of the Scriptural passage (in light of books overall theme) you are reading.*
2. What is the author's point in this Scriptural passage?
3. What does this Scriptural passage teach us about God, man, salvation, and life?
4. How do I apply the truth in this Scriptural passage to my life?

MEMORIZE THE SCRIPTURE (2 MINUTES)

Genesis 1:1
1 In the beginning, God created the heavens and the earth.

DOCTRINES OF SCRIPTURE (2 MINUTES)

What are angels?

Spiritual beings that God created to serve and worship Him (Psalm 148:2, Isaiah 6:2).

SING SCRIPTURAL TRUTH (3 MINUTES)

Amazing Grace (Lyrics in Appendix 1)

PRAY THE TRUTH (3 MINUTES)

- *Praise*
- *Petition*
- *Thank*

Day 10

READ THE SCRIPTURE (5 MINUTES)

Pray for God to grant understanding of the passage of Scripture then read out loud the passage of Scripture in the book of the Bible you are going through verse-by-verse as a family.

DISCUSS THE SCRIPTURE (5 MINUTES)

Four Questions:

1. Who wrote this Biblical book, to whom was it written, and what is the book's main theme? *Always ask this question as it reminds everyone how to approach the examination of the Scriptural passage (in light of books overall theme) you are reading.*
2. What is the author's point in this Scriptural passage?
3. What does this Scriptural passage teach us about God, man, salvation, and life?
4. How do I apply the truth in this Scriptural passage to my life?

MEMORIZE THE SCRIPTURE (2 MINUTES)

Genesis 1:1
1 In the beginning, God created the heavens and the earth.*
Each family member is to recite this Scripture from memory today.

DOCTRINES OF SCRIPTURE (2 MINUTES)

What are demons?

Spiritual beings created to serve God that rebelled against God and where cast down from their glorious state into a forever-fallen state of ruin (Jude 1:6, Ephesians 6:12, 2 Peter 2:4).

SING SCRIPTURAL TRUTH (3 MINUTES)

Amazing Grace (Lyrics in Appendix 1)

PRAY THE TRUTH (3 MINUTES)

- *Praise*
- *Petition*
- *Thank*

Day 11

READ THE SCRIPTURE (5 MINUTES)

Pray for God to grant understanding of the passage of Scripture then read out loud the passage of Scripture in the book of the Bible you are going through verse-by-verse as a family.

DISCUSS THE SCRIPTURE (5 MINUTES)

Four Questions:

1. Who wrote this Biblical book, to whom was it written, and what is the book's main theme? *Always ask this question as it reminds everyone how to approach the examination of the Scriptural passage (in light of books overall theme) you are reading.*
2. What is the author's point in this Scriptural passage?
3. What does this Scriptural passage teach us about God, man, salvation, and life?
4. How do I apply the truth in this Scriptural passage to my life?

MEMORIZE THE SCRIPTURE (2 MINUTES)

John 1:1
1 In the beginning was the Word, and the Word was with God, and the Word was God.

DAY 11

Scripture to recite from memory by a different family member each day:
Genesis 1:1
1 In the beginning, God created the heavens and the earth.

DOCTRINES OF SCRIPTURE (2 MINUTES)

What is total depravity?

All human beings inherit Adam's sin nature and guilt (Romans 5:12, Genesis 3–6).

Mankind's will, mind, and affections are in bondage to sin unable to love God or know Him apart from a work of grace enacted upon the sinner by the Holy Spirit (Romans 1:18–31, Romans 6:20, Romans 3:10–23, Ephesians 2:1–3).

SING SCRIPTURAL TRUTH (3 MINUTES)

Holy, Holy, Holy, Lord God Almighty (Lyrics in Appendix 2)

PRAY THE TRUTH (3 MINUTES)

- *Praise*
- *Petition*
- *Thank*

Day 12

READ THE SCRIPTURE (5 MINUTES)

Pray for God to grant understanding of the passage of Scripture then read out loud the passage of Scripture in the book of the Bible you are going through verse-by-verse as a family.

DISCUSS THE SCRIPTURE (5 MINUTES)

Four Questions:

1. Who wrote this Biblical book, to whom was it written, and what is the book's main theme? *Always ask this question as it reminds everyone how to approach the examination of the Scriptural passage (in light of books overall theme) you are reading.*
2. What is the author's point in this Scriptural passage?
3. What does this Scriptural passage teach us about God, man, salvation, and life?
4. How do I apply the truth in this Scriptural passage to my life?

MEMORIZE THE SCRIPTURE (2 MINUTES)

John 1:1
1 In the beginning was the Word, and the Word was with God, and the Word was God.

Scripture to recite from memory by a different family member each day:
Genesis 1:1
1 In the beginning, God created the heavens and the earth.

DOCTRINES OF SCRIPTURE (2 MINUTES)

What are the four institutions that God created for human flourishing?

1. *Conscience* (Genesis 1:27, Romans 1:19–20, Romans 2:14–16)
2. *Family* (Genesis 2:24, Ephesians 5:21–33)
3. *Government* (Romans 13:1–5, 1 Peter 2:13–17, Mark 12:13–17)
4. *Church* (Matthew 16:18, 1 Timothy 3:15)

SING SCRIPTURAL TRUTH (3 MINUTES)

Holy, Holy, Holy, Lord God Almighty (Lyrics in Appendix 2)

PRAY THE TRUTH (3 MINUTES)

- *Praise*
- *Petition*
- *Thank*

Day 13

READ THE SCRIPTURE (5 MINUTES)

Pray for God to grant understanding of the passage of Scripture then read out loud the passage of Scripture in the book of the Bible you are going through verse-by-verse as a family.

DISCUSS THE SCRIPTURE (5 MINUTES)

Four Questions:

1. Who wrote this Biblical book, to whom was it written, and what is the book's main theme? *Always ask this question as it reminds everyone how to approach the examination of the Scriptural passage (in light of books overall theme) you are reading.*
2. What is the author's point in this Scriptural passage?
3. What does this Scriptural passage teach us about God, man, salvation, and life?
4. How do I apply the truth in this Scriptural passage to my life?

MEMORIZE THE SCRIPTURE (2 MINUTES)

John 1:1
1 In the beginning was the Word, and the Word was with God, and the Word was God.

Scripture to recite from memory by a different family member each day:
Genesis 1:1
1 In the beginning, God created the heavens and the earth.

DOCTRINES OF SCRIPTURE (2 MINUTES)

Who is Jesus?

Jesus is truly God and truly sinless man. He was born of the virgin Mary. He lived a perfect, sinless life by obeying all of God's Law both actively and passively. He died on a cross for the sins of God's people. He was buried. He rose from the dead on the third day, and went back to heaven forty days later. He and God the Father sent the Holy Spirit. He will return someday to judge the living and the dead. All who turn from sin and trust in the Lord Jesus alone will be saved from the judgment of God for their sin. (Matthew—Revelation)

SING SCRIPTURAL TRUTH (3 MINUTES)

Holy, Holy, Holy, Lord God Almighty (Lyrics in Appendix 2)

PRAY THE TRUTH (3 MINUTES)

- *Praise*
- *Petition*
- *Thank*

Day 14

READ THE SCRIPTURE (5 MINUTES)

Pray for God to grant understanding of the passage of Scripture then read out loud the passage of Scripture in the book of the Bible you are going through verse-by-verse as a family.

DISCUSS THE SCRIPTURE (5 MINUTES)

Four Questions:

1. Who wrote this Biblical book, to whom was it written, and what is the book's main theme? *Always ask this question as it reminds everyone how to approach the examination of the Scriptural passage (in light of books overall theme) you are reading.*
2. What is the author's point in this Scriptural passage?
3. What does this Scriptural passage teach us about God, man, salvation, and life?
4. How do I apply the truth in this Scriptural passage to my life?

MEMORIZE THE SCRIPTURE (2 MINUTES)

John 1:1
1 In the beginning was the Word, and the Word was with God, and the Word was God.

Scripture to recite from memory by a different family member each day:
Genesis 1:1
1 In the beginning, God created the heavens and the earth.

DOCTRINES OF SCRIPTURE (2 MINUTES)

What is salvation?

God's gracious and kind work of saving sinners from His wrath and judgment through the life, death, resurrection, and ascension of the Lord Jesus (1 Peter 1:18–19, Romans 8:26–30).

SING SCRIPTURAL TRUTH (3 MINUTES)

Holy, Holy, Holy, Lord God Almighty (Lyrics in Appendix 2)

PRAY THE TRUTH (3 MINUTES)

- *Praise*
- *Petition*
- *Thank*

Day 15

READ THE SCRIPTURE (5 MINUTES)

Pray for God to grant understanding of the passage of Scripture then read out loud the passage of Scripture in the book of the Bible you are going through verse-by-verse as a family.

DISCUSS THE SCRIPTURE (5 MINUTES)

Four Questions:

1. Who wrote this Biblical book, to whom was it written, and what is the book's main theme? *Always ask this question as it reminds everyone how to approach the examination of the Scriptural passage (in light of books overall theme) you are reading.*
2. What is the author's point in this Scriptural passage?
3. What does this Scriptural passage teach us about God, man, salvation, and life?
4. How do I apply the truth in this Scriptural passage to my life?

MEMORIZE THE SCRIPTURE (2 MINUTES)

John 1:1
1 In the beginning was the Word, and the Word was with God, and the Word was God.

DAY 15

Scripture to recite from memory by a different family member each day:
Genesis 1:1
1 In the beginning, God created the heavens and the earth.

DOCTRINES OF SCRIPTURE (2 MINUTES)

What is election?
God chose a people for salvation in Christ Jesus before time began
(Romans 9, Ephesians 1:4–6).

SING SCRIPTURAL TRUTH (3 MINUTES)

Holy, Holy, Holy, Lord God Almighty (Lyrics in Appendix 2)

PRAY THE TRUTH (3 MINUTES)

- *Praise*
- *Petition*
- *Thank*

Day 16

READ THE SCRIPTURE (5 MINUTES)

Pray for God to grant understanding of the passage of Scripture then read out loud the passage of Scripture in the book of the Bible you are going through verse-by-verse as a family.

DISCUSS THE SCRIPTURE (5 MINUTES)

Four Questions:

1. Who wrote this Biblical book, to whom was it written, and what is the book's main theme? *Always ask this question as it reminds everyone how to approach the examination of the Scriptural passage (in light of books overall theme) you are reading.*
2. What is the author's point in this Scriptural passage?
3. What does this Scriptural passage teach us about God, man, salvation, and life?
4. How do I apply the truth in this Scriptural passage to my life?

MEMORIZE THE SCRIPTURE (2 MINUTES)

John 1:1

1 In the beginning was the Word, and the Word was with God, and the Word was God.

Scripture to recite from memory by a different family member each day:
Genesis 1:1
1 In the beginning, God created the heavens and the earth.

DOCTRINES OF SCRIPTURE (2 MINUTES)

What is atonement?

Jesus' sacrifice covers the sin and guilt of God's people (Isaiah 53, 1 John 2:2).

SING SCRIPTURAL TRUTH (3 MINUTES)

Holy, Holy, Holy, Lord God Almighty (Lyrics in Appendix 2)

PRAY THE TRUTH (3 MINUTES)

- *Praise*
- *Petition*
- *Thank*

Day 17

READ THE SCRIPTURE (5 MINUTES)

Pray for God to grant understanding of the passage of Scripture then read out loud the passage of Scripture in the book of the Bible you are going through verse-by-verse as a family.

DISCUSS THE SCRIPTURE (5 MINUTES)

Four Questions:

1. Who wrote this Biblical book, to whom was it written, and what is the book's main theme? *Always ask this question as it reminds everyone how to approach the examination of the Scriptural passage (in light of books overall theme) you are reading.*
2. What is the author's point in this Scriptural passage?
3. What does this Scriptural passage teach us about God, man, salvation, and life?
4. How do I apply the truth in this Scriptural passage to my life?

MEMORIZE THE SCRIPTURE (2 MINUTES)

John 1:1
1 In the beginning was the Word, and the Word was with God, and the Word was God.

Scripture to recite from memory by a different family member each day:
Genesis 1:1
1 In the beginning, God created the heavens and the earth.

DOCTRINES OF SCRIPTURE (2 MINUTES)

What is regeneration?

God the Holy Spirit produces spiritual life in the spiritually dead heart of a person, bringing them to repentance of sin and faith in the Lord Jesus (Ephesians 2:1–8).

SING SCRIPTURAL TRUTH (3 MINUTES)

Holy, Holy, Holy, Lord God Almighty (Lyrics in Appendix 2)

PRAY THE TRUTH (3 MINUTES)

- *Praise*
- *Petition*
- *Thank*

Day 18

Pray for God to grant understanding of the passage of Scripture then read out loud the passage of Scripture in the book of the Bible you are going through verse-by-verse as a family.

DISCUSS THE SCRIPTURE (5 MINUTES)

Four Questions:

1. Who wrote this Biblical book, to whom was it written, and what is the book's main theme? *Always ask this question as it reminds everyone how to approach the examination of the Scriptural passage (in light of books overall theme) you are reading.*
2. What is the author's point in this Scriptural passage?
3. What does this Scriptural passage teach us about God, man, salvation, and life?
4. How do I apply the truth in this Scriptural passage to my life?

MEMORIZE THE SCRIPTURE (2 MINUTES)

John 1:1

1 In the beginning was the Word, and the Word was with God, and the Word was God.

Scripture to recite from memory by a different family member each day:
Genesis 1:1
1 In the beginning, God created the heavens and the earth.

DOCTRINES OF SCRIPTURE (2 MINUTES)

What is adoption?

Having been brought into God's family through the work of the Lord Jesus (Ephesians 1:5).

SING SCRIPTURAL TRUTH (3 MINUTES)

Holy, Holy, Holy, Lord God Almighty (Lyrics in Appendix 2)

PRAY THE TRUTH (3 MINUTES)

- *Praise*
- *Petition*
- *Thank*

Day 19

READ THE SCRIPTURE (5 MINUTES)

Pray for God to grant understanding of the passage of Scripture then read out loud the passage of Scripture in the book of the Bible you are going through verse-by-verse as a family.

DISCUSS THE SCRIPTURE (5 MINUTES)

Four Questions:

1. Who wrote this Biblical book, to whom was it written, and what is the book's main theme? *Always ask this question as it reminds everyone how to approach the examination of the Scriptural passage (in light of books overall theme) you are reading.*
2. What is the author's point in this Scriptural passage?
3. What does this Scriptural passage teach us about God, man, salvation, and life?
4. How do I apply the truth in this Scriptural passage to my life?

MEMORIZE THE SCRIPTURE (2 MINUTES)

John 1:1
1 In the beginning was the Word, and the Word was with God, and the Word was God.

Scripture to recite from memory by a different family member each day:
Genesis 1:1
1 In the beginning, God created the heavens and the earth.

DOCTRINES OF SCRIPTURE (2 MINUTES)

What is justification?

Having been declared right with God through the life and death of Jesus (Romans 3:21–26, 2 Corinthians 5:21).

SING SCRIPTURAL TRUTH (3 MINUTES)

Holy, Holy, Holy, Lord God Almighty (Lyrics in Appendix 2)

PRAY THE TRUTH (3 MINUTES)

- *Praise*
- *Petition*
- *Thank*

Day 20

READ THE SCRIPTURE (5 MINUTES)

Pray for God to grant understanding of the passage of Scripture then read out loud the passage of Scripture in the book of the Bible you are going through verse-by-verse as a family.

DISCUSS THE SCRIPTURE (5 MINUTES)

Four Questions:

1. Who wrote this Biblical book, to whom was it written, and what is the book's main theme? *Always ask this question as it reminds everyone how to approach the examination of the Scriptural passage (in light of books overall theme) you are reading.*
2. What is the author's point in this Scriptural passage?
3. What does this Scriptural passage teach us about God, man, salvation, and life?
4. How do I apply the truth in this Scriptural passage to my life?

MEMORIZE THE SCRIPTURE (2 MINUTES)

John 1:1
1 In the beginning was the Word, and the Word was with God, and the Word was God.
Each family member is to recite this Scripture from memory today

DAY 20

Scripture to recite from memory by a different family member each day:
Genesis 1:1
1 In the beginning, God created the heavens and the earth.

DOCTRINES OF SCRIPTURE (2 MINUTES)

What is sanctification?

Continuously being made more like Jesus each day by the work of the Holy Spirit (John 17:17, Romans 8:9–10, Ezekiel 36:26–27).

SING SCRIPTURAL TRUTH (3 MINUTES)

Holy, Holy, Holy, Lord God Almighty (Lyrics in Appendix 2)

PRAY THE TRUTH (3 MINUTES)

- *Praise*
- *Petition*
- *Thank*

Day 21

READ THE SCRIPTURE (5 MINUTES)

Pray for God to grant understanding of the passage of Scripture then read out loud the passage of Scripture in the book of the Bible you are going through verse-by-verse as a family.

DISCUSS THE SCRIPTURE (5 MINUTES)

Four Questions:

1. Who wrote this Biblical book, to whom was it written, and what is the book's main theme? *Always ask this question as it reminds everyone how to approach the examination of the Scriptural passage (in light of books overall theme) you are reading.*
2. What is the author's point in this Scriptural passage?
3. What does this Scriptural passage teach us about God, man, salvation, and life?
4. How do I apply the truth in this Scriptural passage to my life?

MEMORIZE THE SCRIPTURE (2 MINUTES)

Romans 3:23
[23] for all have sinned and fall short of the glory of God,

Scripture to recite from memory by a different family member each day:
John 1:1
1 In the beginning was the Word, and the Word was with God, and the Word was God.
Genesis 1:1
1 In the beginning, God created the heavens and the earth.

DOCTRINES OF SCRIPTURE (2 MINUTES)

What is glorification?

At the return of Christ, the redeemed will be perfected in body and soul in the image of Christ Jesus (Romans 8:29–30).

SING SCRIPTURAL TRUTH (3 MINUTES)

Doxology (Lyrics in Appendix 3)

PRAY THE TRUTH (3 MINUTES)

- *Praise*
- *Petition*
- *Thank*

Day 22

READ THE SCRIPTURE (5 MINUTES)

Pray for God to grant understanding of the passage of Scripture then read out loud the passage of Scripture in the book of the Bible you are going through verse-by-verse as a family.

DISCUSS THE SCRIPTURE (5 MINUTES)

Four Questions:

1. Who wrote this Biblical book, to whom was it written, and what is the book's main theme? *Always ask this question as it reminds everyone how to approach the examination of the Scriptural passage (in light of books overall theme) you are reading.*
2. What is the author's point in this Scriptural passage?
3. What does this Scriptural passage teach us about God, man, salvation, and life?
4. How do I apply the truth in this Scriptural passage to my life?

MEMORIZE THE SCRIPTURE (2 MINUTES)

Romans 3:23
[23] for all have sinned and fall short of the glory of God,

Scripture to recite from memory by a different family member each day:
John 1:1
1 In the beginning was the Word, and the Word was with God, and the Word was God.
Genesis 1:1
1 In the beginning, God created the heavens and the earth.

DOCTRINES OF SCRIPTURE (2 MINUTES)

What is repentance and faith?

Repentance—A complete change of mind about our sin that produces a turning from sin to Christ Jesus.

Faith—A complete trust in the person and work of the Lord Jesus alone for the forgiveness of sin and eternal life.

(Mark 1:15, Acts 16:31, Acts 5:31)

SING SCRIPTURAL TRUTH (3 MINUTES)

Doxology (Lyrics in Appendix 3)

PRAY THE TRUTH (3 MINUTES)

- *Praise*
- *Petition*
- *Thank*

Day 23

READ THE SCRIPTURE (5 MINUTES)

Pray for God to grant understanding of the passage of Scripture then read out loud the passage of Scripture in the book of the Bible you are going through verse-by-verse as a family.

DISCUSS THE SCRIPTURE (5 MINUTES)

Four Questions:

1. Who wrote this Biblical book, to whom was it written, and what is the book's main theme? *Always ask this question as it reminds everyone how to approach the examination of the Scriptural passage (in light of books overall theme) you are reading.*
2. What is the author's point in this Scriptural passage?
3. What does this Scriptural passage teach us about God, man, salvation, and life?
4. How do I apply the truth in this Scriptural passage to my life?

MEMORIZE THE SCRIPTURE (2 MINUTES)

Romans 3:23
[23] for all have sinned and fall short of the glory of God,

DAY 23

Scripture to recite from memory by a different family member each day:
John 1:1
1 In the beginning was the Word, and the Word was with God, and the Word was God.
Genesis 1:1
1 In the beginning, God created the heavens and the earth.

DOCTRINES OF SCRIPTURE (2 MINUTES)

What is perseverance of the saints?

All those who are saved by God in Christ Jesus will endure in faith to the end (Matthew 24:13, John 10:27–30).

SING SCRIPTURAL TRUTH (3 MINUTES)

Doxology (Lyrics in Appendix 3)

PRAY THE TRUTH (3 MINUTES)

- *Praise*
- *Petition*
- *Thank*

Day 24

READ THE SCRIPTURE (5 MINUTES)

Pray for God to grant understanding of the passage of Scripture then read out loud the passage of Scripture in the book of the Bible you are going through verse-by-verse as a family.

DISCUSS THE SCRIPTURE (5 MINUTES)

Four Questions:

1. Who wrote this Biblical book, to whom was it written, and what is the book's main theme? *Always ask this question as it reminds everyone how to approach the examination of the Scriptural passage (in light of books overall theme) you are reading.*
2. What is the author's point in this Scriptural passage?
3. What does this Scriptural passage teach us about God, man, salvation, and life?
4. How do I apply the truth in this Scriptural passage to my life?

MEMORIZE THE SCRIPTURE (2 MINUTES)

Romans 3:23
23 for all have sinned and fall short of the glory of God,

Day 24

Scripture to recite from memory by a different family member each day:

John 1:1
1 In the beginning was the Word, and the Word was with God, and the Word was God.

Genesis 1:1
1 In the beginning, God created the heavens and the earth.

DOCTRINES OF SCRIPTURE (2 MINUTES)

What are the general call and the effectual call of God?

General call—The Gospel call for all to repent and believe (Acts 17:30).

Effectual call—God's inward call to those whom He set His love on before time, whereby they will come to faith in Christ Jesus (John 6:44).

SING SCRIPTURAL TRUTH (3 MINUTES)

Doxology (Lyrics in Appendix 3)

PRAY THE TRUTH (3 MINUTES)

- *Praise*
- *Petition*
- *Thank*

Day 25

READ THE SCRIPTURE (5 MINUTES)

Pray for God to grant understanding of the passage of Scripture then read out loud the passage of Scripture in the book of the Bible you are going through verse-by-verse as a family.

DISCUSS THE SCRIPTURE (5 MINUTES)

Four Questions:

1. Who wrote this Biblical book, to whom was it written, and what is the book's main theme? *Always ask this question as it reminds everyone how to approach the examination of the Scriptural passage (in light of books overall theme) you are reading.*
2. What is the author's point in this Scriptural passage?
3. What does this Scriptural passage teach us about God, man, salvation, and life?
4. How do I apply the truth in this Scriptural passage to my life?

MEMORIZE THE SCRIPTURE (2 MINUTES)

Romans 3:23
[23] for all have sinned and fall short of the glory of God,

Scripture to recite from memory by a different family member each day:
John 1:1
1 In the beginning was the Word, and the Word was with God, and the Word was God.
Genesis 1:1
1 In the beginning, God created the heavens and the earth.

DOCTRINES OF SCRIPTURE (2 MINUTES)

What is the kingdom of God?
God's sovereign reign over His redeemed people both now and into the final state, as well as His sovereign reign over all mankind unto the end of His perfect judgment that will be dispensed in the final state against all those in rebellion to His rule (Matthew 4:17, John 18:36, 1 Corinthians 15:25, Revelation 19–22).

SING SCRIPTURAL TRUTH (3 MINUTES)

Doxology (Lyrics in Appendix 3)

PRAY THE TRUTH (3 MINUTES)

- *Praise*
- *Petition*
- *Thank*

Day 26

READ THE SCRIPTURE (5 MINUTES)

Pray for God to grant understanding of the passage of Scripture then read out loud the passage of Scripture in the book of the Bible you are going through verse-by-verse as a family.

DISCUSS THE SCRIPTURE (5 MINUTES)

Four Questions:

1. Who wrote this Biblical book, to whom was it written, and what is the book's main theme? *Always ask this question as it reminds everyone how to approach the examination of the Scriptural passage (in light of books overall theme) you are reading.*
2. What is the author's point in this Scriptural passage?
3. What does this Scriptural passage teach us about God, man, salvation, and life?
4. How do I apply the truth in this Scriptural passage to my life?

MEMORIZE THE SCRIPTURE (2 MINUTES)

Romans 3:23
[23] for all have sinned and fall short of the glory of God,

Scripture to recite from memory by a different family member each day:
John 1:1
1 In the beginning was the Word, and the Word was with God, and the Word was God.
Genesis 1:1
1 In the beginning, God created the heavens and the earth.

DOCTRINES OF SCRIPTURE (2 MINUTES)

What is the universal (catholic) church?

All of the redeemed of Christ Jesus from all ages in time (1 Corinthians 12:13, Colossians 1:18).

SING SCRIPTURAL TRUTH (3 MINUTES)

Doxology (Lyrics in Appendix 3)

PRAY THE TRUTH (3 MINUTES)

- *Praise*
- *Petition*
- *Thank*

Day 27

READ THE SCRIPTURE (5 MINUTES)

Pray for God to grant understanding of the passage of Scripture then read out loud the passage of Scripture in the book of the Bible you are going through verse-by-verse as a family.

DISCUSS THE SCRIPTURE (5 MINUTES)

Four Questions:

1. Who wrote this Biblical book, to whom was it written, and what is the book's main theme? *Always ask this question as it reminds everyone how to approach the examination of the Scriptural passage (in light of books overall theme) you are reading.*
2. What is the author's point in this Scriptural passage?
3. What does this Scriptural passage teach us about God, man, salvation, and life?
4. How do I apply the truth in this Scriptural passage to my life?

MEMORIZE THE SCRIPTURE (2 MINUTES)

Romans 3:23
[23] for all have sinned and fall short of the glory of God,

Scripture to recite from memory by a different family member each day:
John 1:1
1 In the beginning was the Word, and the Word was with God, and the Word was God.
Genesis 1:1
1 In the beginning, God created the heavens and the earth.

DOCTRINES OF SCRIPTURE (2 MINUTES)

What is the local church?

A local gathering (body) of God's redeemed who gather each Lord's day around the Word preached, read, sung, and prayed as well as ordinances properly practiced.

The two ordinances of a local church are baptism and the Lord's Supper (communion).

(1 Corinthians 1:2, Acts 20:28, Hebrews 10:24–25)

SING SCRIPTURAL TRUTH (3 MINUTES)

Doxology (Lyrics in Appendix 3)

PRAY THE TRUTH (3 MINUTES)

- *Praise*
- *Petition*
- *Thank*

Day 28

READ THE SCRIPTURE (5 MINUTES)

Pray for God to grant understanding of the passage of Scripture then read out loud the passage of Scripture in the book of the Bible you are going through verse-by-verse as a family.

DISCUSS THE SCRIPTURE (5 MINUTES)

Four Questions:

1. Who wrote this Biblical book, to whom was it written, and what is the book's main theme? *Always ask this question as it reminds everyone how to approach the examination of the Scriptural passage (in light of books overall theme) you are reading.*
2. What is the author's point in this Scriptural passage?
3. What does this Scriptural passage teach us about God, man, salvation, and life?
4. How do I apply the truth in this Scriptural passage to my life?

MEMORIZE THE SCRIPTURE (2 MINUTES)

Romans 3:23
[23] for all have sinned and fall short of the glory of God,

Scripture to recite from memory by a different family member each day:
John 1:1
1 In the beginning was the Word, and the Word was with God, and the Word was God.
Genesis 1:1
1 In the beginning, God created the heavens and the earth.

DOCTRINES OF SCRIPTURE (2 MINUTES)

What is the final state for Christians and non-Christians?

The Christian's final state is eternal joy on the New Earth as a perfected soul in a glorified body (1 Thessalonians 4, Revelation 21–22).

The non-Christian's final state is eternal judgment in the lake of fire as a depraved soul in a body enduring eternal torment (Revelation 20).

SING SCRIPTURAL TRUTH (3 MINUTES)

Doxology (Lyrics in Appendix 3)

PRAY THE TRUTH (3 MINUTES)

- *Praise*
- *Petition*
- *Thank*

Day 29

READ THE SCRIPTURE (5 MINUTES)

Pray for God to grant understanding of the passage of Scripture then read out loud the passage of Scripture in the book of the Bible you are going through verse-by-verse as a family.

DISCUSS THE SCRIPTURE (5 MINUTES)

Four Questions:

1. Who wrote this Biblical book, to whom was it written, and what is the book's main theme? *Always ask this question as it reminds everyone how to approach the examination of the Scriptural passage (in light of books overall theme) you are reading.*
2. What is the author's point in this Scriptural passage?
3. What does this Scriptural passage teach us about God, man, salvation, and life?
4. How do I apply the truth in this Scriptural passage to my life?

MEMORIZE THE SCRIPTURE (2 MINUTES)

Romans 3:23
[23] for all have sinned and fall short of the glory of God,

Scripture to recite from memory by a different family member each day:
John 1:1
1 In the beginning was the Word, and the Word was with God, and the Word was God.
Genesis 1:1
1 In the beginning, God created the heavens and the earth.

DOCTRINES OF SCRIPTURE (2 MINUTES)

What are first four commandments of the Ten Commandments (summarized)?

1. Do not have any other gods before me (the LORD).
2. Do not make idols of any kind.
3. Do not take the name of the LORD your God in vain.
4. Remember the Sabbath day to keep it holy.
   (Exodus 20:1–20)

SING SCRIPTURAL TRUTH (3 MINUTES)

Doxology (Lyrics in Appendix 3)

PRAY THE TRUTH (3 MINUTES)

- *Praise*
- *Petition*
- *Thank*

Day 30

READ THE SCRIPTURE (5 MINUTES)

Pray for God to grant understanding of the passage of Scripture then read out loud the passage of Scripture in the book of the Bible you are going through verse-by-verse as a family.

DISCUSS THE SCRIPTURE (5 MINUTES)

Four Questions:

1. Who wrote this Biblical book, to whom was it written, and what is the book's main theme? *Always ask this question as it reminds everyone how to approach the examination of the Scriptural passage (in light of books overall theme) you are reading.*
2. What is the author's point in this Scriptural passage?
3. What does this Scriptural passage teach us about God, man, salvation, and life?
4. How do I apply the truth in this Scriptural passage to my life?

MEMORIZE THE SCRIPTURE (2 MINUTES)

Romans 3:23
²³ for all have sinned and fall short of the glory of God, *
Each family member is to recite this Scripture from memory today.

Scripture to recite from memory by a different family member each day:
John 1:1
1 In the beginning was the Word, and the Word was with God, and the Word was God.
Genesis 1:1
1 In the beginning, God created the heavens and the earth.

DOCTRINES OF SCRIPTURE (2 MINUTES)

What are the last six of the Ten Commandments (summarized)?
5. Honor your father and mother.
6. Do not murder.
7. Do not commit adultery.
8. Do not steal.
9. Do not lie.
10. Do not covet.
    (Exodus 20:1–20)

SING SCRIPTURAL TRUTH (3 MINUTES)

Doxology (Lyrics in Appendix 3)

PRAY THE TRUTH (3 MINUTES)

- *Praise*
- *Petition*
- *Thank*

Day 31

READ THE SCRIPTURE (5 MINUTES)

Pray for God to grant understanding of the passage of Scripture then read out loud the passage of Scripture in the book of the Bible you are going through verse-by-verse as a family.

DISCUSS THE SCRIPTURE (5 MINUTES)

Four Questions:

1. Who wrote this Biblical book, to whom was it written, and what is the book's main theme? *Always ask this question as it reminds everyone how to approach the examination of the Scriptural passage (in light of books overall theme) you are reading.*
2. What is the author's point in this Scriptural passage?
3. What does this Scriptural passage teach us about God, man, salvation, and life?
4. How do I apply the truth in this Scriptural passage to my life?

MEMORIZE THE SCRIPTURE (2 MINUTES)

Romans 6:23
23 For the wages of sin is death, but the free gift of God is eternal life in Christ Jesus our Lord.

Scripture to recite from memory by a different family member each day:
Romans 3:23
[23] for all have sinned and fall short of the glory of God,
John 1:1
1 In the beginning was the Word, and the Word was with God, and the Word was God.
Genesis 1:1
1 In the beginning, God created the heavens and the earth.

DOCTRINES OF SCRIPTURE (2 MINUTES)

What is the Bible?

The Bible is the inspired, authoritative Word of God. *(2 Timothy 3:16–17)*

The Bible, in its original autographs, is without error in all that it teaches. *(Old Testament—Hebrew and little Aramaic, New Testament—Greek)*

SING SCRIPTURAL TRUTH (3 MINUTES)

Be Thou My Vision (Lyrics in Appendix 4)

PRAY THE TRUTH (3 MINUTES)

- *Praise*
- *Petition*
- *Thank*

Day 32

READ THE SCRIPTURE (5 MINUTES)

Pray for God to grant understanding of the passage of Scripture then read out loud the passage of Scripture in the book of the Bible you are going through verse-by-verse as a family.

DISCUSS THE SCRIPTURE (5 MINUTES)

Four Questions:

1. Who wrote this Biblical book, to whom was it written, and what is the book's main theme? *Always ask this question as it reminds everyone how to approach the examination of the Scriptural passage (in light of books overall theme) you are reading.*
2. What is the author's point in this Scriptural passage?
3. What does this Scriptural passage teach us about God, man, salvation, and life?
4. How do I apply the truth in this Scriptural passage to my life?

MEMORIZE THE SCRIPTURE (2 MINUTES)

Romans 6:23
23 For the wages of sin is death, but the free gift of God is eternal life in Christ Jesus our Lord.

Scripture to recite from memory by a different family member each day:
Romans 3:23
[23] for all have sinned and fall short of the glory of God,
John 1:1
1 In the beginning was the Word, and the Word was with God, and the Word was God.
Genesis 1:1
1 In the beginning, God created the heavens and the earth.

DOCTRINES OF SCRIPTURE (2 MINUTES)

What is a Biblical Covenant?

A Biblical covenant is an agreement between God and man. Or an agreement within the Triune God Himself *(Covenant of Redemption)*.

There are seven covenants recorded in Holy Scripture. See Appendix 7 for descriptions of the covenants.

(Genesis—Revelation)

SING SCRIPTURAL TRUTH (3 MINUTES)

Be Thou My Vision (Lyrics in Appendix 4)

PRAY THE TRUTH (3 MINUTES)

- *Praise*
- *Petition*
- *Thank*

Day 33

READ THE SCRIPTURE (5 MINUTES)

Pray for God to grant understanding of the passage of Scripture then read out loud the passage of Scripture in the book of the Bible you are going through verse-by-verse as a family.

DISCUSS THE SCRIPTURE (5 MINUTES)

Four Questions:

1. Who wrote this Biblical book, to whom was it written, and what is the book's main theme? *Always ask this question as it reminds everyone how to approach the examination of the Scriptural passage (in light of books overall theme) you are reading.*
2. What is the author's point in this Scriptural passage?
3. What does this Scriptural passage teach us about God, man, salvation, and life?
4. How do I apply the truth in this Scriptural passage to my life?

MEMORIZE THE SCRIPTURE (2 MINUTES)

Romans 6:23
23 For the wages of sin is death, but the free gift of God is eternal life in Christ Jesus our Lord.

Scripture to recite from memory by a different family member each day:
Romans 3:23
²³ for all have sinned and fall short of the glory of God,
John 1:1
1 In the beginning was the Word, and the Word was with God, and the Word was God.
Genesis 1:1
1 In the beginning, God created the heavens and the earth.

DOCTRINES OF SCRIPTURE (2 MINUTES)

What are the covenants of the Bible?

Covenant of Redemption *(Ephesians 1:3–14)*, Adamic Covenant *(Genesis 2:15–17)*, Noahic Covenant *(Genesis 8:20–9:17)*, Abrahamic Covenant *(Genesis 12:1–3, Genesis 13:14–18, Genesis 15, Genesis 17)*, Mosaic Covenant *(Exodus 20—Deuteronomy 34)*, Davidic Covenant *(2 Samuel 7)*, New Covenant *(Matthew—Revelation)*.

SING SCRIPTURAL TRUTH (3 MINUTES)

Be Thou My Vision (Lyrics in Appendix 4)

PRAY THE TRUTH (3 MINUTES)

- *Praise*
- *Petition*
- *Thank*

Day 34

READ THE SCRIPTURE (5 MINUTES)

Pray for God to grant understanding of the passage of Scripture then read out loud the passage of Scripture in the book of the Bible you are going through verse-by-verse as a family.

DISCUSS THE SCRIPTURE (5 MINUTES)

Four Questions:

1. Who wrote this Biblical book, to whom was it written, and what is the book's main theme? *Always ask this question as it reminds everyone how to approach the examination of the Scriptural passage (in light of books overall theme) you are reading.*
2. What is the author's point in this Scriptural passage?
3. What does this Scriptural passage teach us about God, man, salvation, and life?
4. How do I apply the truth in this Scriptural passage to my life?

MEMORIZE THE SCRIPTURE (2 MINUTES)

Romans 6:23
23 For the wages of sin is death, but the free gift of God is eternal life in Christ Jesus our Lord.

Scripture to recite from memory by a different family member each day:
Romans 3:23
²³ for all have sinned and fall short of the glory of God,
John 1:1
1 In the beginning was the Word, and the Word was with God, and the Word was God.
Genesis 1:1
1 In the beginning, God created the heavens and the earth.

DOCTRINES OF SCRIPTURE (2 MINUTES)

Who is God?

God is One God, Three Eternally Distinct Persons. Father, Son, and Holy Spirit.

God is the Holy Creator and Sovereign Ruler of heaven and earth.

(John 1:1–4, Matthew 28:18–20, Genesis 1:1–2).

SING SCRIPTURAL TRUTH (3 MINUTES)

Be Thou My Vision (Lyrics in Appendix 4)

PRAY THE TRUTH (3 MINUTES)

- *Praise*
- *Petition*
- *Thank*

Day 35

READ THE SCRIPTURE (5 MINUTES)

Pray for God to grant understanding of the passage of Scripture then read out loud the passage of Scripture in the book of the Bible you are going through verse-by-verse as a family.

DISCUSS THE SCRIPTURE (5 MINUTES)

Four Questions:

1. Who wrote this Biblical book, to whom was it written, and what is the book's main theme? *Always ask this question as it reminds everyone how to approach the examination of the Scriptural passage (in light of books overall theme) you are reading.*
2. What is the author's point in this Scriptural passage?
3. What does this Scriptural passage teach us about God, man, salvation, and life?
4. How do I apply the truth in this Scriptural passage to my life?

MEMORIZE THE SCRIPTURE (2 MINUTES)

Romans 6:23
23 For the wages of sin is death, but the free gift of God is eternal life in Christ Jesus our Lord.

Scripture to recite from memory by a different family member each day:
Romans 3:23
[23] for all have sinned and fall short of the glory of God,
John 1:1
1 In the beginning was the Word, and the Word was with God, and the Word was God.
Genesis 1:1
1 In the beginning, God created the heavens and the earth.

DOCTRINES OF SCRIPTURE (2 MINUTES)

What are God's attributes?

God's attributes are His characteristics.

God is: Triune (One God, Three Persons), Love, Eternal, Omniscient (All Knowing), Omnipotent (All Powerful), Omnipresent (Fully everywhere at all times), Holy, Just, Righteous, Pure, Faithful, True, Merciful, Perfect in all His characteristics.

(Genesis—Revelation)

SING SCRIPTURAL TRUTH (3 MINUTES)

Be Thou My Vision (Lyrics in Appendix 4)

PRAY THE TRUTH (3 MINUTES)

- *Praise*
- *Petition*
- *Thank*

Day 36

READ THE SCRIPTURE (5 MINUTES)

Pray for God to grant understanding of the passage of Scripture then read out loud the passage of Scripture in the book of the Bible you are going through verse-by-verse as a family.

DISCUSS THE SCRIPTURE (5 MINUTES)

Four Questions:

1. Who wrote this Biblical book, to whom was it written, and what is the book's main theme? *Always ask this question as it reminds everyone how to approach the examination of the Scriptural passage (in light of books overall theme) you are reading.*
2. What is the author's point in this Scriptural passage?
3. What does this Scriptural passage teach us about God, man, salvation, and life?
4. How do I apply the truth in this Scriptural passage to my life?

MEMORIZE THE SCRIPTURE (2 MINUTES)

Romans 6:23
23 For the wages of sin is death, but the free gift of God is eternal life in Christ Jesus our Lord.

Scripture to recite from memory by a different family member each day:
Romans 3:23
[23] for all have sinned and fall short of the glory of God,
John 1:1
1 In the beginning was the Word, and the Word was with God, and the Word was God.
Genesis 1:1
1 In the beginning, God created the heavens and the earth.

DOCTRINES OF SCRIPTURE (2 MINUTES)

What is Creation?

Creation includes all of the universe and everything within it. This includes the galaxies, earth, and all of its creatures which God created and continues to sustain (Psalm 104).

SING SCRIPTURAL TRUTH (3 MINUTES)

Be Thou My Vision (Lyrics in Appendix 4)

PRAY THE TRUTH (3 MINUTES)

- *Praise*
- *Petition*
- *Thank*

Day 37

READ THE SCRIPTURE (5 MINUTES)

Pray for God to grant understanding of the passage of Scripture then read out loud the passage of Scripture in the book of the Bible you are going through verse-by-verse as a family.

DISCUSS THE SCRIPTURE (5 MINUTES)

Four Questions:

1. Who wrote this Biblical book, to whom was it written, and what is the book's main theme? *Always ask this question as it reminds everyone how to approach the examination of the Scriptural passage (in light of books overall theme) you are reading.*
2. What is the author's point in this Scriptural passage?
3. What does this Scriptural passage teach us about God, man, salvation, and life?
4. How do I apply the truth in this Scriptural passage to my life?

MEMORIZE THE SCRIPTURE (2 MINUTES)

Romans 6:23
23 For the wages of sin is death, but the free gift of God is eternal life in Christ Jesus our Lord.

Scripture to recite from memory by a different family member each day:
Romans 3:23
²³ for all have sinned and fall short of the glory of God,
John 1:1
1 In the beginning was the Word, and the Word was with God, and the Word was God.
Genesis 1:1
1 In the beginning, God created the heavens and the earth.

DOCTRINES OF SCRIPTURE (2 MINUTES)

What is the pinnacle of God's creation?

Man and woman is the pinnacle of God's creation as those made in the image of God (Genesis 1:26–27).

SING SCRIPTURAL TRUTH (3 MINUTES)

Be Thou My Vision (Lyrics in Appendix 4)

PRAY THE TRUTH (3 MINUTES)

- *Praise*
- *Petition*
- *Thank*

Day 38

READ THE SCRIPTURE (5 MINUTES)

Pray for God to grant understanding of the passage of Scripture then read out loud the passage of Scripture in the book of the Bible you are going through verse-by-verse as a family.

DISCUSS THE SCRIPTURE (5 MINUTES)

Four Questions:

1. Who wrote this Biblical book, to whom was it written, and what is the book's main theme? *Always ask this question as it reminds everyone how to approach the examination of the Scriptural passage (in light of books overall theme) you are reading.*
2. What is the author's point in this Scriptural passage?
3. What does this Scriptural passage teach us about God, man, salvation, and life?
4. How do I apply the truth in this Scriptural passage to my life?

MEMORIZE THE SCRIPTURE (2 MINUTES)

Romans 6:23
23 For the wages of sin is death, but the free gift of God is eternal life in Christ Jesus our Lord.

Scripture to recite from memory by a different family member each day:
Romans 3:23
²³ for all have sinned and fall short of the glory of God,
John 1:1
1 In the beginning was the Word, and the Word was with God, and the Word was God.
Genesis 1:1
1 In the beginning, God created the heavens and the earth.

DOCTRINES OF SCRIPTURE (2 MINUTES)

What is marriage?
God created marriage as one man and one woman in a covenant relationship as husband and wife, forsaking all others (Genesis 2:24).
Marriage is a picture of the Gospel (Ephesians 5:21–33).

SING SCRIPTURAL TRUTH (3 MINUTES)

Be Thou My Vision (Lyrics in Appendix 4)

PRAY THE TRUTH (3 MINUTES)

- *Praise*
- *Petition*
- *Thank*

Day 39

READ THE SCRIPTURE (5 MINUTES)

Pray for God to grant understanding of the passage of Scripture then read out loud the passage of Scripture in the book of the Bible you are going through verse-by-verse as a family.

DISCUSS THE SCRIPTURE (5 MINUTES)

Four Questions:

1. Who wrote this Biblical book, to whom was it written, and what is the book's main theme? *Always ask this question as it reminds everyone how to approach the examination of the Scriptural passage (in light of books overall theme) you are reading.*
2. What is the author's point in this Scriptural passage?
3. What does this Scriptural passage teach us about God, man, salvation, and life?
4. How do I apply the truth in this Scriptural passage to my life?

MEMORIZE THE SCRIPTURE (2 MINUTES)

Romans 6:23
23 For the wages of sin is death, but the free gift of God is eternal life in Christ Jesus our Lord.

Scripture to recite from memory by a different family member each day:
Romans 3:23
²³ for all have sinned and fall short of the glory of God,
John 1:1
1 In the beginning was the Word, and the Word was with God, and the Word was God.
Genesis 1:1
1 In the beginning, God created the heavens and the earth.

DOCTRINES OF SCRIPTURE (2 MINUTES)

What are angels?

Spiritual beings that God created to serve and worship Him (Psalm 148:2, Isaiah 6:2).

SING SCRIPTURAL TRUTH (3 MINUTES)

Be Thou My Vision (Lyrics in Appendix 4)

PRAY THE TRUTH (3 MINUTES)

- *Praise*
- *Petition*
- *Thank*

Day 40

READ THE SCRIPTURE (5 MINUTES)

Pray for God to grant understanding of the passage of Scripture then read out loud the passage of Scripture in the book of the Bible you are going through verse-by-verse as a family.

DISCUSS THE SCRIPTURE (5 MINUTES)

Four Questions:

1. Who wrote this Biblical book, to whom was it written, and what is the book's main theme? *Always ask this question as it reminds everyone how to approach the examination of the Scriptural passage (in light of books overall theme) you are reading.*
2. What is the author's point in this Scriptural passage?
3. What does this Scriptural passage teach us about God, man, salvation, and life?
4. How do I apply the truth in this Scriptural passage to my life?

MEMORIZE THE SCRIPTURE (2 MINUTES)

Romans 6:23
23 For the wages of sin is death, but the free gift of God is eternal life in Christ Jesus our Lord. *
Each family member is to recite this Scripture from memory today.

Scripture to recite from memory by a different family member each day:
Romans 3:23
²³ for all have sinned and fall short of the glory of God,
John 1:1
1 In the beginning was the Word, and the Word was with God, and the Word was God.
Genesis 1:1
1 In the beginning, God created the heavens and the earth.

DOCTRINES OF SCRIPTURE (2 MINUTES)

What are demons?

Spiritual beings created to serve God, that rebelled against God and where cast down from their glorious state into a forever fallen state of ruin (Jude 1:6, Ephesians 6:12, 2 Peter 2:4).

SING SCRIPTURAL TRUTH (3 MINUTES)

Be Thou My Vision (Lyrics in Appendix 4)

PRAY THE TRUTH (3 MINUTES)

- *Praise*
- *Petition*
- *Thank*

Day 41

READ THE SCRIPTURE (5 MINUTES)

Pray for God to grant understanding of the passage of Scripture then read out loud the passage of Scripture in the book of the Bible you are going through verse-by-verse as a family.

DISCUSS THE SCRIPTURE (5 MINUTES)

Four Questions:

1. Who wrote this Biblical book, to whom was it written, and what is the book's main theme? *Always ask this question as it reminds everyone how to approach the examination of the Scriptural passage (in light of books overall theme) you are reading.*
2. What is the author's point in this Scriptural passage?
3. What does this Scriptural passage teach us about God, man, salvation, and life?
4. How do I apply the truth in this Scriptural passage to my life?

MEMORIZE THE SCRIPTURE (2 MINUTES)

John 3:16
[16] For God so loved the world, that he gave his only Son, that whoever believes in him should not perish but have eternal life.

Scripture to recite from memory by a different family member each day:
Romans 6:23
23 For the wages of sin is death, but the free gift of God is eternal life in Christ Jesus our Lord
Romans 3:23
[23] for all have sinned and fall short of the glory of God,
John 1:1
1 In the beginning was the Word, and the Word was with God, and the Word was God.
Genesis 1:1
1 In the beginning, God created the heavens and the earth.

DOCTRINES OF SCRIPTURE (2 MINUTES)

What is total depravity?

All human beings inherit Adam's sin nature and guilt (Romans 5:12, Genesis 3–6).

Mankind's will, mind, and affections are in bondage to sin unable to love God or know Him apart from a work of grace enacted upon the sinner by the Holy Spirit (Romans 1:18–31, Romans 6:20, Romans 3:10–23, Ephesians 2:1–3).

SING SCRIPTURAL TRUTH (3 MINUTES)

Mighty Fortress is our God (Lyrics in Appendix 5)

PRAY THE TRUTH (3 MINUTES)

- *Praise*
- *Petition*
- *Thank*

Day 42

READ THE SCRIPTURE (5 MINUTES)

Pray for God to grant understanding of the passage of Scripture then read out loud the passage of Scripture in the book of the Bible you are going through verse-by-verse as a family.

DISCUSS THE SCRIPTURE (5 MINUTES)

Four Questions:

1. Who wrote this Biblical book, to whom was it written, and what is the book's main theme? *Always ask this question as it reminds everyone how to approach the examination of the Scriptural passage (in light of books overall theme) you are reading.*
2. What is the author's point in this Scriptural passage?
3. What does this Scriptural passage teach us about God, man, salvation, and life?
4. How do I apply the truth in this Scriptural passage to my life?

MEMORIZE THE SCRIPTURE (2 MINUTES)

John 3:16
[16] For God so loved the world, that he gave his only Son, that whoever believes in him should not perish but have eternal life.

Scripture to recite from memory by a different family member each day:
Romans 6:23
23 For the wages of sin is death, but the free gift of God is eternal life in Christ Jesus our Lord
Romans 3:23
[23] for all have sinned and fall short of the glory of God,
John 1:1
1 In the beginning was the Word, and the Word was with God, and the Word was God.
Genesis 1:1
1 In the beginning, God created the heavens and the earth.

DOCTRINES OF SCRIPTURE (2 MINUTES)

What are the four institutions that God created for human flourishing?

1. *Conscience* (Genesis 1:27, Romans 1:19–20, Romans 2:14–16)
2. *Family* (Genesis 2:24, Ephesians 5:21–33)
3. *Government* (Romans 13:1–5, 1 Peter 2:13–17, Mark 12:13–17)
4. *Church* (Matthew 16:18, 1 Timothy 3:15)

SING SCRIPTURAL TRUTH (3 MINUTES)

Mighty Fortress is our God (Lyrics in Appendix 5)

PRAY THE TRUTH (3 MINUTES)

- *Praise*
- *Petition*
- *Thank*

Day 43

READ THE SCRIPTURE (5 MINUTES)

Pray for God to grant understanding of the passage of Scripture then read out loud the passage of Scripture in the book of the Bible you are going through verse-by-verse as a family.

DISCUSS THE SCRIPTURE (5 MINUTES)

Four Questions:

1. Who wrote this Biblical book, to whom was it written, and what is the book's main theme? *Always ask this question as it reminds everyone how to approach the examination of the Scriptural passage (in light of books overall theme) you are reading.*
2. What is the author's point in this Scriptural passage?
3. What does this Scriptural passage teach us about God, man, salvation, and life?
4. How do I apply the truth in this Scriptural passage to my life?

MEMORIZE THE SCRIPTURE (2 MINUTES)

John 3:16
[16] For God so loved the world, that he gave his only Son, that whoever believes in him should not perish but have eternal life.

Scripture to recite from memory by a different family member each day:
Romans 6:23
23 For the wages of sin is death, but the free gift of God is eternal life in Christ Jesus our Lord
Romans 3:23
[23] for all have sinned and fall short of the glory of God,
John 1:1
1 In the beginning was the Word, and the Word was with God, and the Word was God.
Genesis 1:1
1 In the beginning, God created the heavens and the earth.

DOCTRINES OF SCRIPTURE (2 MINUTES)

Who is Jesus?

Jesus is truly God and truly sinless man. Born of the virgin Mary. He lived a perfect, sinless life obeying all of God's Law both actively and passively. He died on a cross for the sins of God's people. He was buried. He rose from the dead on the third day, and went back to heaven forty days later. He and God the Father sent the Holy Spirit. He will return someday to judge the living and the dead. All who turn from sin and trust in the Lord Jesus alone will be saved from the judgment of God and their sin.

(Matthew—Revelation)

SING SCRIPTURAL TRUTH (3 MINUTES)

Mighty Fortress is our God (Lyrics in Appendix 5)

PRAY THE TRUTH (3 MINUTES)

- *Praise*
- *Petition*
- *Thank*

Day 44

READ THE SCRIPTURE (5 MINUTES)

Pray for God to grant understanding of the passage of Scripture then read out loud the passage of Scripture in the book of the Bible you are going through verse-by-verse as a family.

DISCUSS THE SCRIPTURE (5 MINUTES)

Four Questions:

1. Who wrote this Biblical book, to whom was it written, and what is the book's main theme? *Always ask this question as it reminds everyone how to approach the examination of the Scriptural passage (in light of books overall theme) you are reading.*
2. What is the author's point in this Scriptural passage?
3. What does this Scriptural passage teach us about God, man, salvation, and life?
4. How do I apply the truth in this Scriptural passage to my life?

MEMORIZE THE SCRIPTURE (2 MINUTES)

John 3:16
16 For God so loved the world, that he gave his only Son, that whoever believes in him should not perish but have eternal life.

Scripture to recite from memory by a different family member each day:
Romans 6:23
23 For the wages of sin is death, but the free gift of God is eternal life in Christ Jesus our Lord
Romans 3:23
[23] for all have sinned and fall short of the glory of God,
John 1:1
1 In the beginning was the Word, and the Word was with God, and the Word was God.
Genesis 1:1
1 In the beginning, God created the heavens and the earth.

DOCTRINES OF SCRIPTURE (2 MINUTES)

What is salvation?

God's gracious and kind work of saving sinners from His wrath and judgment through the life, death, resurrection, and ascension of the Lord Jesus (1 Peter 1:18–19, Romans 8:26–30).

SING SCRIPTURAL TRUTH (3 MINUTES)

Mighty Fortress is our God (Lyrics in Appendix 5)

PRAY THE TRUTH (3 MINUTES)

- *Praise*
- *Petition*
- *Thank*

Day 45

READ THE SCRIPTURE (5 MINUTES)

Pray for God to grant understanding of the passage of Scripture then read out loud the passage of Scripture in the book of the Bible you are going through verse-by-verse as a family.

DISCUSS THE SCRIPTURE (5 MINUTES)

Four Questions:

1. Who wrote this Biblical book, to whom was it written, and what is the book's main theme? *Always ask this question as it reminds everyone how to approach the examination of the Scriptural passage (in light of books overall theme) you are reading.*
2. What is the author's point in this Scriptural passage?
3. What does this Scriptural passage teach us about God, man, salvation, and life?
4. How do I apply the truth in this Scriptural passage to my life?

MEMORIZE THE SCRIPTURE (2 MINUTES)

John 3:16
[16] For God so loved the world, that he gave his only Son, that whoever believes in him should not perish but have eternal life.

DAY 45

Scripture to recite from memory by a different family member each day:
Romans 6:23
23 For the wages of sin is death, but the free gift of God is eternal life in Christ Jesus our Lord
Romans 3:23
²³ for all have sinned and fall short of the glory of God,
John 1:1
1 In the beginning was the Word, and the Word was with God, and the Word was God.
Genesis 1:1
1 In the beginning, God created the heavens and the earth.

DOCTRINES OF SCRIPTURE (2 MINUTES)

What is election?

God chose a people for salvation in Christ Jesus before time began (Romans 9, Ephesians 1:4–6).

SING SCRIPTURAL TRUTH (3 MINUTES)

Mighty Fortress is our God (Lyrics in Appendix 5)

PRAY THE TRUTH (3 MINUTES)

- *Praise*
- *Petition*
- *Thank*

Day 46

READ THE SCRIPTURE (5 MINUTES)

Pray for God to grant understanding of the passage of Scripture then read out loud the passage of Scripture in the book of the Bible you are going through verse-by-verse as a family.

DISCUSS THE SCRIPTURE (5 MINUTES)

Four Questions:

1. Who wrote this Biblical book, to whom was it written, and what is the book's main theme? *Always ask this question as it reminds everyone how to approach the examination of the Scriptural passage (in light of books overall theme) you are reading.*
2. What is the author's point in this Scriptural passage?
3. What does this Scriptural passage teach us about God, man, salvation, and life?
4. How do I apply the truth in this Scriptural passage to my life?

MEMORIZE THE SCRIPTURE (2 MINUTES)

John 3:16
[16] For God so loved the world, that he gave his only Son, that whoever believes in him should not perish but have eternal life.

Scripture to recite from memory by a different family member each day:
Romans 6:23

23 For the wages of sin is death, but the free gift of God is eternal life in Christ Jesus our Lord

Romans 3:23

23 for all have sinned and fall short of the glory of God,

John 1:1

1 In the beginning was the Word, and the Word was with God, and the Word was God.

Genesis 1:1

1 In the beginning, God created the heavens and the earth.

DOCTRINES OF SCRIPTURE (2 MINUTES)

What is atonement?

Jesus' sacrifice covers the sin and guilt of God's people (Isaiah 53, 1 John 2:2).

SING SCRIPTURAL TRUTH (3 MINUTES)

Mighty Fortress is our God (Lyrics in Appendix 5)

PRAY THE TRUTH (3 MINUTES)

- *Praise*
- *Petition*
- *Thank*

Day 47

READ THE SCRIPTURE (5 MINUTES)

Pray for God to grant understanding of the passage of Scripture then read out loud the passage of Scripture in the book of the Bible you are going through verse-by-verse as a family.

DISCUSS THE SCRIPTURE (5 MINUTES)

Four Questions:

1. Who wrote this Biblical book, to whom was it written, and what is the book's main theme? *Always ask this question as it reminds everyone how to approach the examination of the Scriptural passage (in light of books overall theme) you are reading.*
2. What is the author's point in this Scriptural passage?
3. What does this Scriptural passage teach us about God, man, salvation, and life?
4. How do I apply the truth in this Scriptural passage to my life?

MEMORIZE THE SCRIPTURE (2 MINUTES)

John 3:16
[16] For God so loved the world, that he gave his only Son, that whoever believes in him should not perish but have eternal life.

DAY 47

Scripture to recite from memory by a different family member each day:
Romans 6:23
23 For the wages of sin is death, but the free gift of God is eternal life in Christ Jesus our Lord
Romans 3:23
23 for all have sinned and fall short of the glory of God,
John 1:1
1 In the beginning was the Word, and the Word was with God, and the Word was God.
Genesis 1:1
1 In the beginning, God created the heavens and the earth.

DOCTRINES OF SCRIPTURE (2 MINUTES)

What is regeneration?

God the Holy Spirit produces spiritual life in the spiritually dead heart of a person bringing them to repentance of sin and faith in the Lord Jesus (Ephesians 2:1–8).

SING SCRIPTURAL TRUTH (3 MINUTES)

Mighty Fortress is our God (Lyrics in Appendix 5)

PRAY THE TRUTH (3 MINUTES)

- *Praise*
- *Petition*
- *Thank*

Day 48

READ THE SCRIPTURE (5 MINUTES)

Pray for God to grant understanding of the passage of Scripture then read out loud the passage of Scripture in the book of the Bible you are going through verse-by-verse as a family.

DISCUSS THE SCRIPTURE (5 MINUTES)

Four Questions:

1. Who wrote this Biblical book, to whom was it written, and what is the book's main theme? *Always ask this question as it reminds everyone how to approach the examination of the Scriptural passage (in light of books overall theme) you are reading.*
2. What is the author's point in this Scriptural passage?
3. What does this Scriptural passage teach us about God, man, salvation, and life?
4. How do I apply the truth in this Scriptural passage to my life?

MEMORIZE THE SCRIPTURE (2 MINUTES)

John 3:16
[16] For God so loved the world, that he gave his only Son, that whoever believes in him should not perish but have eternal life.

Scripture to recite from memory by a different family member each day:
Romans 6:23
23 For the wages of sin is death, but the free gift of God is eternal life in Christ Jesus our Lord
Romans 3:23
[23] for all have sinned and fall short of the glory of God,
John 1:1
1 In the beginning was the Word, and the Word was with God, and the Word was God.
Genesis 1:1
1 In the beginning, God created the heavens and the earth.

DOCTRINES OF SCRIPTURE (2 MINUTES)

What is adoption?
Having been brought into God's family through the work of the Lord Jesus (Ephesians 1:5).

SING SCRIPTURAL TRUTH (3 MINUTES)

Mighty Fortress is our God (Lyrics in Appendix 5)

PRAY THE TRUTH (3 MINUTES)

- *Praise*
- *Petition*
- *Thank*

Day 49

READ THE SCRIPTURE (5 MINUTES)

Pray for God to grant understanding of the passage of Scripture then read out loud the passage of Scripture in the book of the Bible you are going through verse-by-verse as a family.

DISCUSS THE SCRIPTURE (5 MINUTES)

Four Questions:

1. Who wrote this Biblical book, to whom was it written, and what is the book's main theme? *Always ask this question as it reminds everyone how to approach the examination of the Scriptural passage (in light of books overall theme) you are reading.*
2. What is the author's point in this Scriptural passage?
3. What does this Scriptural passage teach us about God, man, salvation, and life?
4. How do I apply the truth in this Scriptural passage to my life?

MEMORIZE THE SCRIPTURE (2 MINUTES)

John 3:16
[16] For God so loved the world, that he gave his only Son, that whoever believes in him should not perish but have eternal life.

Scripture to recite from memory by a different family member each day:
Romans 6:23
23 For the wages of sin is death, but the free gift of God is eternal life in Christ Jesus our Lord
Romans 3:23
[23] for all have sinned and fall short of the glory of God,
John 1:1
1 In the beginning was the Word, and the Word was with God, and the Word was God.
Genesis 1:1
1 In the beginning, God created the heavens and the earth.

DOCTRINES OF SCRIPTURE (2 MINUTES)

What is justification?

Having been declared right with God through the life and death of Jesus (Romans 3:21–26, 2 Corinthians 5:21).

SING SCRIPTURAL TRUTH (3 MINUTES)

Mighty Fortress is our God (Lyrics in Appendix 5)

PRAY THE TRUTH (3 MINUTES)

- *Praise*
- *Petition*
- *Thank*

Day 50

READ THE SCRIPTURE (5 MINUTES)

Pray for God to grant understanding of the passage of Scripture then read out loud the passage of Scripture in the book of the Bible you are going through verse-by-verse as a family.

DISCUSS THE SCRIPTURE (5 MINUTES)

Four Questions:

1. Who wrote this Biblical book, to whom was it written, and what is the book's main theme? *Always ask this question as it reminds everyone how to approach the examination of the Scriptural passage (in light of books overall theme) you are reading.*
2. What is the author's point in this Scriptural passage?
3. What does this Scriptural passage teach us about God, man, salvation, and life?
4. How do I apply the truth in this Scriptural passage to my life?

MEMORIZE THE SCRIPTURE (2 MINUTES)

John 3:16
16 For God so loved the world, that he gave his only Son, that whoever believes in him should not perish but have eternal life.*
*Each family member is to recite this Scripture from memory today

DAY 50

Scripture to recite from memory by a different family member each day:
Romans 6:23
23 For the wages of sin is death, but the free gift of God is eternal life in Christ Jesus our Lord
Romans 3:23
[23] for all have sinned and fall short of the glory of God,
John 1:1
1 In the beginning was the Word, and the Word was with God, and the Word was God.
Genesis 1:1
1 In the beginning, God created the heavens and the earth.

DOCTRINES OF SCRIPTURE (2 MINUTES)

What is sanctification?

Continuously being made more like Jesus each day by the work of the Holy Spirit (John 17:17, Romans 8:9–10, Ezekiel 36:26–27).

SING SCRIPTURAL TRUTH (3 MINUTES)

Mighty Fortress is our God (Lyrics in Appendix 5)

PRAY THE TRUTH (3 MINUTES)

- *Praise*
- *Petition*
- *Thank*

Day 51

READ THE SCRIPTURE (5 MINUTES)

Pray for God to grant understanding of the passage of Scripture then read out loud the passage of Scripture in the book of the Bible you are going through verse-by-verse as a family.

DISCUSS THE SCRIPTURE (5 MINUTES)

Four Questions:

1. Who wrote this Biblical book, to whom was it written, and what is the book's main theme? *Always ask this question as it reminds everyone how to approach the examination of the Scriptural passage (in light of books overall theme) you are reading.*
2. What is the author's point in this Scriptural passage?
3. What does this Scriptural passage teach us about God, man, salvation, and life?
4. How do I apply the truth in this Scriptural passage to my life?

MEMORIZE THE SCRIPTURE (2 MINUTES)

Ephesians 2:8–9
[8] For by grace you have been saved through faith. And this is not your own doing; it is the gift of God, [9] not a result of works, so that no one may boast.

Scripture to recite from memory by a different family member each day:
John 3:16

¹⁶ For God so loved the world, that he gave his only Son, that whoever believes in him should not perish but have eternal life

Romans 6:23

23 For the wages of sin is death, but the free gift of God is eternal life in Christ Jesus our Lord

Romans 3:23

²³ for all have sinned and fall short of the glory of God,

John 1:1

1 In the beginning was the Word, and the Word was with God, and the Word was God.

Genesis 1:1

1 In the beginning, God created the heavens and the earth.

DOCTRINES OF SCRIPTURE (2 MINUTES)

What is glorification?

At the return of Christ, the redeemed will be perfected in body and soul in the image of Christ Jesus (Romans 8:29–30).

SING SCRIPTURAL TRUTH (3 MINUTES)

This is My Father's World (Lyrics in Appendix 6)

PRAY THE TRUTH (3 MINUTES)

- *Praise*
- *Petition*
- *Thank*

Day 52

READ THE SCRIPTURE (5 MINUTES)

Pray for God to grant understanding of the passage of Scripture then read out loud the passage of Scripture in the book of the Bible you are going through verse-by-verse as a family.

DISCUSS THE SCRIPTURE (5 MINUTES)

Four Questions:

1. Who wrote this Biblical book, to whom was it written, and what is the book's main theme? *Always ask this question as it reminds everyone how to approach the examination of the Scriptural passage (in light of books overall theme) you are reading.*
2. What is the author's point in this Scriptural passage?
3. What does this Scriptural passage teach us about God, man, salvation, and life?
4. How do I apply the truth in this Scriptural passage to my life?

MEMORIZE THE SCRIPTURE (2 MINUTES)

Ephesians 2:8–9

[8] For by grace you have been saved through faith. And this is not your own doing; it is the gift of God. [9] not a result of works, so that no one may boast.

Scripture to recite from memory by a different family member each day:
John 3:16

[16] For God so loved the world, that he gave his only Son, that whoever believes in him should not perish but have eternal life

Romans 6:23

23 For the wages of sin is death, but the free gift of God is eternal life in Christ Jesus our Lord

Romans 3:23

[23] for all have sinned and fall short of the glory of God,

John 1:1

1 In the beginning was the Word, and the Word was with God, and the Word was God.

Genesis 1:1

1 In the beginning, God created the heavens and the earth.

DOCTRINES OF SCRIPTURE (2 MINUTES)

What are repentance and faith?

Repentance—A complete change of mind about our sin that produces a turning from sin to Christ Jesus.

Faith—A complete trust in the person and work of the Lord Jesus alone for the forgiveness of sin and eternal life.

(Mark 1:15, Acts 16:31, Acts 5:31)

SING SCRIPTURAL TRUTH (3 MINUTES)

This is My Father's World (Lyrics in Appendix 6)

PRAY THE TRUTH (3 MINUTES)

- *Praise*
- *Petition*
- *Thank*

Day 53

READ THE SCRIPTURE (5 MINUTES)

Pray for God to grant understanding of the passage of Scripture then read out loud the passage of Scripture in the book of the Bible you are going through verse-by-verse as a family.

DISCUSS THE SCRIPTURE (5 MINUTES)

Four Questions:

1. Who wrote this Biblical book, to whom was it written, and what is the book's main theme? *Always ask this question as it reminds everyone how to approach the examination of the Scriptural passage (in light of books overall theme) you are reading.*
2. What is the author's point in this Scriptural passage?
3. What does this Scriptural passage teach us about God, man, salvation, and life?
4. How do I apply the truth in this Scriptural passage to my life?

MEMORIZE THE SCRIPTURE (2 MINUTES)

Ephesians 2:8–9

[8] For by grace you have been saved through faith. And this is not your own doing; it is the gift of God, [9] not a result of works, so that no one may boast.

Scripture to recite from memory by a different family member each day:
John 3:16
[16] For God so loved the world, that he gave his only Son, that whoever believes in him should not perish but have eternal life
Romans 6:23
23 For the wages of sin is death, but the free gift of God is eternal life in Christ Jesus our Lord
Romans 3:23
[23] for all have sinned and fall short of the glory of God,
John 1:1
1 In the beginning was the Word, and the Word was with God, and the Word was God.
Genesis 1:1
1 In the beginning, God created the heavens and the earth.

DOCTRINES OF SCRIPTURE (2 MINUTES)

What is perseverance of the saints?

All those saved by God in Christ Jesus will endure in faith to the end (Matthew 24:13, John 10:27–30).

SING SCRIPTURAL TRUTH (3 MINUTES)

This is My Father's World (Lyrics in Appendix 6)

PRAY THE TRUTH (3 MINUTES)

- *Praise*
- *Petition*
- *Thank*

Day 54

READ THE SCRIPTURE (5 MINUTES)

Pray for God to grant understanding of the passage of Scripture then read out loud the passage of Scripture in the book of the Bible you are going through verse-by-verse as a family.

DISCUSS THE SCRIPTURE (5 MINUTES)

Four Questions:

1. Who wrote this Biblical book, to whom was it written, and what is the book's main theme? *Always ask this question as it reminds everyone how to approach the examination of the Scriptural passage (in light of books overall theme) you are reading.*
2. What is the author's point in this Scriptural passage?
3. What does this Scriptural passage teach us about God, man, salvation, and life?
4. How do I apply the truth in this Scriptural passage to my life?

MEMORIZE THE SCRIPTURE (2 MINUTES)

Ephesians 2:8–9

[8] For by grace you have been saved through faith. And this is not your own doing; it is the gift of God, [9] not a result of works, so that no one may boast.

Scripture to recite from memory by a different family member each day:
John 3:16
[16] For God so loved the world, that he gave his only Son, that whoever believes in him should not perish but have eternal life
Romans 6:23
23 For the wages of sin is death, but the free gift of God is eternal life in Christ Jesus our Lord
Romans 3:23
[23] for all have sinned and fall short of the glory of God,
John 1:1
1 In the beginning was the Word, and the Word was with God, and the Word was God.
Genesis 1:1
1 In the beginning, God created the heavens and the earth.

DOCTRINES OF SCRIPTURE (2 MINUTES)

What is the general call of God and effectual call of God?
General call—The Gospel call for all to repent and believe (Acts 17:30).
Effectual call—God's inward call to those whom He has set His love on from before time, whereby they will come to faith in Christ Jesus (John 6:44).

SING SCRIPTURAL TRUTH (3 MINUTES)

This is My Father's World (Lyrics in Appendix 6)

PRAY THE TRUTH (3 MINUTES)

- *Praise*
- *Petition*
- *Thank*

Day 55

READ THE SCRIPTURE (5 MINUTES)

Pray for God to grant understanding of the passage of Scripture then read out loud the passage of Scripture in the book of the Bible you are going through verse-by-verse as a family.

DISCUSS THE SCRIPTURE (5 MINUTES)

Four Questions:

1. Who wrote this Biblical book, to whom was it written, and what is the book's main theme? *Always ask this question as it reminds everyone how to approach the examination of the Scriptural passage (in light of books overall theme) you are reading.*
2. What is the author's point in this Scriptural passage?
3. What does this Scriptural passage teach us about God, man, salvation, and life?
4. How do I apply the truth in this Scriptural passage to my life?

MEMORIZE THE SCRIPTURE (2 MINUTES)

Ephesians 2:8–9
[8] For by grace you have been saved through faith. And this is not your own doing; it is the gift of God, [9] not a result of works, so that no one may boast.

Scripture to recite from memory by a different family member each day:
John 3:16

[16] For God so loved the world, that he gave his only Son, that whoever believes in him should not perish but have eternal life
Romans 6:23

23 For the wages of sin is death, but the free gift of God is eternal life in Christ Jesus our Lord
Romans 3:23

[23] for all have sinned and fall short of the glory of God,
John 1:1

1 In the beginning was the Word, and the Word was with God, and the Word was God.
Genesis 1:1

1 In the beginning, God created the heavens and the earth.

DOCTRINES OF SCRIPTURE (2 MINUTES)

What is the kingdom of God?

God's sovereign reign over His redeemed people both now and into the final state, as well as His sovereign reign over all mankind unto the end of His perfect judgment that will be dispensed in the final state against all those in rebellion to His rule (Matthew 4:17, John 18:36, 1 Corinthians 15:25, Revelation 19–22).

SING SCRIPTURAL TRUTH (3 MINUTES)

This is My Father's World (Lyrics in Appendix 6)

PRAY THE TRUTH (3 MINUTES)

- *Praise*
- *Petition*
- *Thank*

Day 56

READ THE SCRIPTURE (5 MINUTES)

Pray for God to grant understanding of the passage of Scripture then read out loud the passage of Scripture in the book of the Bible you are going through verse-by-verse as a family.

DISCUSS THE SCRIPTURE (5 MINUTES)

Four Questions:

1. Who wrote this Biblical book, to whom was it written, and what is the book's main theme? *Always ask this question as it reminds everyone how to approach the examination of the Scriptural passage (in light of books overall theme) you are reading.*
2. What is the author's point in this Scriptural passage?
3. What does this Scriptural passage teach us about God, man, salvation, and life?
4. How do I apply the truth in this Scriptural passage to my life?

MEMORIZE THE SCRIPTURE (2 MINUTES)

Ephesians 2:8–9

[8] For by grace you have been saved through faith. And this is not your own doing; it is the gift of God, [9] not a result of works, so that no one may boast.

Scripture to recite from memory by a different family member each day:
John 3:16
[16] For God so loved the world, that he gave his only Son, that whoever believes in him should not perish but have eternal life
Romans 6:23
23 For the wages of sin is death, but the free gift of God is eternal life in Christ Jesus our Lord
Romans 3:23
[23] for all have sinned and fall short of the glory of God,
John 1:1
1 In the beginning was the Word, and the Word was with God, and the Word was God.
Genesis 1:1
1 In the beginning, God created the heavens and the earth.

DOCTRINES OF SCRIPTURE (2 MINUTES)

What is the universal (catholic) church?
All of the redeemed of Christ Jesus from all ages in time (1 Corinthians 12:13, Colossians 1:18).

SING SCRIPTURAL TRUTH (3 MINUTES)

This is My Father's World (Lyrics in Appendix 6)

PRAY THE TRUTH (3 MINUTES)

- *Praise*
- *Petition*
- *Thank*

Day 57

READ THE SCRIPTURE (5 MINUTES)

Pray for God to grant understanding of the passage of Scripture then read out loud the passage of Scripture in the book of the Bible you are going through verse-by-verse as a family.

DISCUSS THE SCRIPTURE (5 MINUTES)

Four Questions:

1. Who wrote this Biblical book, to whom was it written, and what is the book's main theme? *Always ask this question as it reminds everyone how to approach the examination of the Scriptural passage (in light of books overall theme) you are reading.*
2. What is the author's point in this Scriptural passage?
3. What does this Scriptural passage teach us about God, man, salvation, and life?
4. How do I apply the truth in this Scriptural passage to my life?

MEMORIZE THE SCRIPTURE (2 MINUTES)

Ephesians 2:8–9
[8] For by grace you have been saved through faith. And this is not your own doing; it is the gift of God, [9] not a result of works, so that no one may boast.

DAY 57

Scripture to recite from memory by a different family member each day:
John 3:16

[16] For God so loved the world, that he gave his only Son, that whoever believes in him should not perish but have eternal life
Romans 6:23

23 For the wages of sin is death, but the free gift of God is eternal life in Christ Jesus our Lord
Romans 3:23

[23] for all have sinned and fall short of the glory of God,
John 1:1

1 In the beginning was the Word, and the Word was with God, and the Word was God.
Genesis 1:1

1 In the beginning, God created the heavens and the earth.

DOCTRINES OF SCRIPTURE (2 MINUTES)

What is the local church?

A local gathering (body) of God's redeemed who gather each Lord's day around the Word preached, read, sung, and prayed as well as ordinances properly practiced.

The two ordinances of a local church are baptism and the Lord's Supper (communion).

(1 Corinthians 1:2, Acts 20:28, Hebrews 10:24–25)

SING SCRIPTURAL TRUTH (3 MINUTES)

This is My Father's World (Lyrics in Appendix 6)

PRAY THE TRUTH (3 MINUTES)

- *Praise*
- *Petition*
- *Thank*

Day 58

READ THE SCRIPTURE (5 MINUTES)

Pray for God to grant understanding of the passage of Scripture then read out loud the passage of Scripture in the book of the Bible you are going through verse-by-verse as a family.

DISCUSS THE SCRIPTURE (5 MINUTES)

Four Questions:

1. Who wrote this Biblical book, to whom was it written, and what is the book's main theme? *Always ask this question as it reminds everyone how to approach the examination of the Scriptural passage (in light of books overall theme) you are reading.*
2. What is the author's point in this Scriptural passage?
3. What does this Scriptural passage teach us about God, man, salvation, and life?
4. How do I apply the truth in this Scriptural passage to my life?

MEMORIZE THE SCRIPTURE (2 MINUTES)

Ephesians 2:8–9
[8] For by grace you have been saved through faith. And this is not your own doing; it is the gift of God, [9] not a result of works, so that no one may boast.

Scripture to recite from memory by a different family member each day:
John 3:16
[16] For God so loved the world, that he gave his only Son, that whoever believes in him should not perish but have eternal life
Romans 6:23
23 For the wages of sin is death, but the free gift of God is eternal life in Christ Jesus our Lord
Romans 3:23
[23] for all have sinned and fall short of the glory of God,
John 1:1
1 In the beginning was the Word, and the Word was with God, and the Word was God.
Genesis 1:1
1 In the beginning, God created the heavens and the earth.

DOCTRINES OF SCRIPTURE (2 MINUTES)

What is the final state for Christians and non-Christians?

The Christian's final state is eternal joy on the New Earth as a perfected soul in a glorified body (1 Thessalonians 4, Revelation 21–22).

The non-Christian's final state is eternal judgment in the lake of fire as a depraved soul in a body enduring eternal torment (Revelation 20).

SING SCRIPTURAL TRUTH (3 MINUTES)

This is My Father's World (Lyrics in Appendix 6)

PRAY THE TRUTH (3 MINUTES)

- *Praise*
- *Petition*
- *Thank*

Day 59

READ THE SCRIPTURE (5 MINUTES)

Pray for God to grant understanding of the passage of Scripture then read out loud the passage of Scripture in the book of the Bible you are going through verse-by-verse as a family.

DISCUSS THE SCRIPTURE (5 MINUTES)

Four Questions:

1. Who wrote this Biblical book, to whom was it written, and what is the book's main theme? *Always ask this question as it reminds everyone how to approach the examination of the Scriptural passage (in light of books overall theme) you are reading.*
2. What is the author's point in this Scriptural passage?
3. What does this Scriptural passage teach us about God, man, salvation, and life?
4. How do I apply the truth in this Scriptural passage to my life?

MEMORIZE THE SCRIPTURE (2 MINUTES)

Ephesians 2:8–9
[8] For by grace you have been saved through faith. And this is not your own doing; it is the gift of God, [9] not a result of works, so that no one may boast.

Scripture to recite from memory by a different family member each day:
John 3:16
[16] For God so loved the world, that he gave his only Son, that whoever believes in him should not perish but have eternal life
Romans 6:23
23 For the wages of sin is death, but the free gift of God is eternal life in Christ Jesus our Lord
Romans 3:23
[23] for all have sinned and fall short of the glory of God,
John 1:1
1 In the beginning was the Word, and the Word was with God, and the Word was God.
Genesis 1:1
1 In the beginning, God created the heavens and the earth.

DOCTRINES OF SCRIPTURE (2 MINUTES)

What are first four commandments of the Ten Commandments (summarized)?

1. Do not have any other gods before me (the LORD).
2. Do not make idols of any kind.
3. Do not take the name of the LORD your God in vain.
4. Remember the Sabbath day to keep it holy.

(Exodus 20:1–20)

SING SCRIPTURAL TRUTH (3 MINUTES)

This is My Father's World (Lyrics in Appendix 6)
[A] Pray the Truth (3 Minutes)

- *Praise*
- *Petition*
- *Thank*

Day 60

READ THE SCRIPTURE (5 MINUTES)

Pray for God to grant understanding of the passage of Scripture then read out loud the passage of Scripture in the book of the Bible you are going through verse-by-verse as a family.

DISCUSS THE SCRIPTURE (5 MINUTES)

Four Questions:

1. Who wrote this Biblical book, to whom was it written, and what is the book's main theme? *Always ask this question as it reminds everyone how to approach the examination of the Scriptural passage (in light of books overall theme) you are reading.*
2. What is the author's point in this Scriptural passage?
3. What does this Scriptural passage teach us about God, man, salvation, and life?
4. How do I apply the truth in this Scriptural passage to my life?

MEMORIZE THE SCRIPTURE (2 MINUTES)

Ephesians 2:8–9
[8] For by grace you have been saved through faith. And this is not your own doing; it is the gift of God, [9] not a result of works, so that no one may boast.*
Each family member is to recite this Scripture from memory today.

Scripture to recite from memory by a different family member each day:
John 3:16
¹⁶ For God so loved the world, that he gave his only Son, that whoever believes in him should not perish but have eternal life
Romans 6:23
23 For the wages of sin is death, but the free gift of God is eternal life in Christ Jesus our Lord
Romans 3:23
²³ for all have sinned and fall short of the glory of God,
John 1:1
1 In the beginning was the Word, and the Word was with God, and the Word was God.
Genesis 1:1
1 In the beginning, God created the heavens and the earth.

DOCTRINES OF SCRIPTURE (2 MINUTES)

What are the last six of the Ten Commandments (summarized)?
5. Honor your father and mother.
6. Do not murder.
7. Do not commit adultery.
8. Do not steal.
9. Do not lie.
10. Do not covet.
   (Exodus 20:1–20)

SING SCRIPTURAL TRUTH (3 MINUTES)

This is My Father's World (Lyrics in Appendix 6)

PRAY THE TRUTH (3 MINUTES)

- *Praise*
- *Petition*
- *Thank*

Appendix 1

AMAZING GRACE

1 Amazing grace! how sweet the sound,
That saved a wretch; like me!
I once was lost, but now am found,
Was blind, but now I see.

2 'Twas grace that taught my heart to fear,
And grace my fears relieved;
How precious did that grace appear
The hour I first believed!

3 The Lord hath promised good to me,
His word my hope secures;
He will my shield and portion be
As long as life endures.

4 When we've been there ten thousand years,
Bright shining as the sun,
We've no less days to sing God's praise
Than when we first begun.

Appendix 2

HOLY, HOLY, HOLY, LORD GOD ALMIGHTY

1 Holy, holy, holy! Lord God Almighty!
Early in the morning our song shall rise to thee.
Holy, holy, holy! Merciful and mighty!
God in three Persons, blessed Trinity!

2 Holy, holy, holy! All the saints adore thee,
casting down their golden crowns around the glassy sea;
cherubim and seraphim falling down before thee,
who wert, and art, and evermore shalt be.

3 Holy, holy, holy! Though the darkness hide thee,
though the eye of sinful man thy glory may not see,
only thou art holy; there is none beside thee
perfect in pow'r, in love, and purity.

4 Holy, holy, holy! Lord God Almighty!
All thy works shall praise thy name in earth and sky and sea.
Holy, holy, holy! Merciful and mighty!
God in three Persons, blessed Trinity!

Appendix 3

DOXOLOGY

Praise God, from whom all blessings flow;
Praise Him, all creatures here below;
Praise Him above, ye heav'nly host;
Praise Father, Son, and Holy Ghost.
Amen.

Appendix 4

BE THOU MY VISION

1 Be thou my vision, O Lord of my heart;
naught be all else to me, save that thou art—
thou my best thought by day or by night,
waking or sleeping, thy presence my light.

2 Be thou my wisdom, and thou my true word;
I ever with thee and thou with me, Lord;
thou my great Father, I thy true son;
thou in me dwelling, and I with thee one.

3 Be thou my battle shield, sword for my fight;
be thou my dignity, thou my delight,
thou my soul's shelter, thou my high tow'r:
raise thou me heav'n-ward, O Pow'r of my pow'r.

4 Riches I heed not, nor man's empty praise,
thou mine inheritance, now and always:
thou and thou only, first in my heart,
High King of heaven, my treasure thou art.

5 High King of heaven, my victory won,
may I reach heaven's joys, O bright heav'n's Sun!
Heart of my own heart, whatever befall,
still be my vision, O Ruler of all.

Appendix 5

MIGHTY FORTRESS IS OUR GOD

1 A mighty fortress is our God,
a bulwark never failing;
our helper he, amid the flood
of mortal ills prevailing.
For still our ancient foe
does seek to work us woe;
his craft and power are great,
and armed with cruel hate,
on earth is not his equal.

2 Did we in our own strength confide,
our striving would be losing,
were not the right Man on our side,
the Man of God's own choosing.
You ask who that may be?
Christ Jesus, it is he;
Lord Sabaoth his name,
from age to age the same;
and he must win the battle.

3 And though this world, with devils filled,
should threaten to undo us,
we will not fear, for God has willed
his truth to triumph through us.

The prince of darkness grim,
we tremble not for him;
his rage we can endure,
for lo! his doom is sure;
one little word shall fell him.

4 That Word above all earthly powers
no thanks to them abideth;
the Spirit and the gifts are ours
through him who with us sideth.
Let goods and kindred go,
this mortal life also;
the body they may kill:
God's truth abideth still;
his kingdom is forever!

Appendix 6

THIS IS MY FATHER'S WORLD

1 This is my Father's world,
And to my listening ears
All nature sings, and round me rings
The music of the spheres.
This is my Father's world:
I rest me in the thought
Of rocks and trees, of skies and seas—
His hand the wonders wrought.

2 This is my Father's world:
The birds their carols raise,
The morning light, the lily white,
Declare their Maker's praise.
This is my Father's world:
He shines in all that's fair;
In the rustling grass I hear Him pass,
He speaks to me everywhere.

3 This is my Father's world:
O let me ne'er forget
That though the wrong seems oft so strong,
God is the Ruler yet.
This is my Father's world:
Why should my heart be sad?
The Lord is King: let the heavens ring!
God reigns; let earth be glad!

Appendix 7

COVENANT EXPLANATIONS

Covenant of Redemption—God the Father chose a people. God the Son agreed to redeem them by adding humanity and dying for them. God the Holy Spirit agreed to live in, and sanctify them (Ephesians 1:3–14).

Adamic Covenant—God told Adam to not eat from the tree of the knowledge of good and evil for in the day he did he would die (Genesis 2:15–17).

Noahic Covenant—God told Noah he would not destroy the earth again by water, and that as long as the earth existed all seasons would be kept in place (Genesis 8:20–9:17).

Abrahamic Covenant—God told Abraham He would make him a mighty nation and give his offspring the land of promise. Through his seed all nations of the earth would be blessed (Genesis 12:1–3, Genesis 13:14–18, Genesis 15, Genesis 17).

Mosaic Covenant—God gave Israel His Law and promised that if they obeyed this Law they would be blessed in the land of promise, but if they disobeyed, they would be punished and eventually exiled (Exodus 20—Deuteronomy 34).

Davidic Covenant—God told David that he would establish his son's kingdom and give his house an everlasting kingdom (2 Samuel 7).

New Covenant—God commands all to repent and believe on the Lord Jesus.

The Lord Jesus who is truly God and truly man. He was born of the virgin Mary. He lived a perfect sinless life. He died on the cross for the sins of His people. He was buried. He rose from the dead on the third day and went back to heaven forty days later. God the Father and Jesus sent the Holy Spirit. All who turn from sin and trust in the Lord Jesus will be saved (Matthew—Revelation).

Appendix 8

Creeds *(These creed were developed throughout church history and are very beneficial to learn, as time allows and progress is made in the doctrine section of this family worship methodology)*

APOSTLES CREED

I believe in God, the Father almighty,
 creator of heaven and earth.
I believe in Jesus Christ, his only Son, our Lord,
 who was conceived by the Holy Spirit
 and born of the virgin Mary.
 He suffered under Pontius Pilate,
 was crucified, died, and was buried;
 he descended to hell.
 The third day he rose again from the dead.
 He ascended to heaven
 and is seated at the right hand of God the Father almighty.
 From there he will come to judge the living and the dead.
I believe in the Holy Spirit,
 the holy catholic* church,
 the communion of saints,
 the forgiveness of sins,
 the resurrection of the body,
 and the life everlasting. Amen.[1]

---

1. These Creeds were from the Christian Reformed Church website. https://www.crcna.org/welcome/beliefs/creeds/athanasian-creed?language_content_entity=en. Accessed on 11/12/2020.

NICENE CREED

We believe in one God,
  the Father almighty,
  maker of heaven and earth,
  of all things visible and invisible.
And in one Lord Jesus Christ,
  the only Son of God,
  begotten from the Father before all ages,
    God from God,
    Light from Light,
    true God from true God,
  begotten, not made;
  of the same essence as the Father.
  Through him all things were made.
For us and for our salvation
  he came down from heaven;
  he became incarnate by the Holy Spirit and the virgin Mary,
  and was made human.
  He was crucified for us under Pontius Pilate;
  he suffered and was buried.
  The third day he rose again, according to the Scriptures.
  He ascended to heaven
  and is seated at the right hand of the Father.
  He will come again with glory
  to judge the living and the dead.
  His kingdom will never end.
And we believe in the Holy Spirit,
  the Lord, the giver of life.
  He proceeds from the Father and the Son,
  and with the Father and the Son is worshiped and glorified.
  He spoke through the prophets.
  We believe in one holy catholic and apostolic church.
  We affirm one baptism for the forgiveness of sins.
  We look forward to the resurrection of the dead,
  and to life in the world to come. Amen.[2]

2. These Creeds were from the Christian Reformed Church website.

ATHANASIAN CREED

Whoever desires to be saved should above all hold to the catholic faith.

Anyone who does not keep it whole and unbroken will doubtless perish eternally.

Now this is the catholic faith:

That we worship one God in trinity and the trinity in unity,
neither blending their persons
nor dividing their essence.

For the person of the Father is a distinct person,
the person of the Son is another,
and that of the Holy Spirit still another.

But the divinity of the Father, Son, and Holy Spirit is one,
their glory equal, their majesty coeternal.

What quality the Father has, the Son has, and the Holy Spirit has.

The Father is uncreated,
the Son is uncreated,
the Holy Spirit is uncreated.

The Father is immeasurable,
the Son is immeasurable,
the Holy Spirit is immeasurable.

The Father is eternal,
the Son is eternal,
the Holy Spirit is eternal.

And yet there are not three eternal beings;
there is but one eternal being.

So too there are not three uncreated or immeasurable beings;
there is but one uncreated and immeasurable being.

Similarly, the Father is almighty,
the Son is almighty,
the Holy Spirit is almighty.

Yet there are not three almighty beings;
there is but one almighty being.

Thus the Father is God,

---

https://www.crcna.org/welcome/beliefs/creeds/athanasian-creed?language_content_entity=en. Accessed on 11/12/2020.

the Son is God,
the Holy Spirit is God.
   Yet there are not three gods;
   there is but one God.
Thus the Father is Lord,
the Son is Lord,
the Holy Spirit is Lord.
   Yet there are not three lords;
   there is but one Lord.
Just as Christian truth compels us
to confess each person individually
as both God and Lord,
so catholic religion forbids us
to say that there are three gods or lords.
The Father was neither made nor created nor begotten from anyone.
The Son was neither made nor created;
he was begotten from the Father alone.
The Holy Spirit was neither made nor created nor begotten;
he proceeds from the Father and the Son.
Accordingly there is one Father, not three fathers;
there is one Son, not three sons;
there is one Holy Spirit, not three holy spirits.
Nothing in this trinity is before or after,
nothing is greater or smaller;
in their entirety the three persons
are coeternal and coequal with each other.
So in everything, as was said earlier,
we must worship their trinity in their unity
and their unity in their trinity.
Anyone then who desires to be saved
should think thus about the trinity.
But it is necessary for eternal salvation
that one also believe in the incarnation
of our Lord Jesus Christ faithfully.
Now this is the true faith:
   That we believe and confess
   that our Lord Jesus Christ, God's Son,

is both God and human, equally.
 He is God from the essence of the Father,
begotten before time;
and he is human from the essence of his mother,
born in time;
completely God, completely human,
with a rational soul and human flesh;
equal to the Father as regards divinity,
less than the Father as regards humanity.
Although he is God and human,
yet Christ is not two, but one.
He is one, however,
not by his divinity being turned into flesh,
but by God's taking humanity to himself.
He is one,
certainly not by the blending of his essence,
but by the unity of his person.
For just as one human is both rational soul and flesh,
so too the one Christ is both God and human.
He suffered for our salvation;
he descended to hell;
he arose from the dead;
he ascended to heaven;
he is seated at the Father's right hand;
from there he will come to judge the living and the dead.
At his coming all people will arise bodily
and give an accounting of their own deeds.
Those who have done good will enter eternal life,
and those who have done evil will enter eternal fire.
This is the catholic faith:
one cannot be saved without believing it firmly and faithfully.[3]

3. These Creeds were from the Christian Reformed Church website. https://www.crcna.org/welcome/beliefs/creeds/athanasian-creed?language_content_entity=en. Accessed on 11/12/2020.

www.ingramcontent.com/pod-product-compliance
Lightning Source LLC
Chambersburg PA
CBHW070449090426
42735CB00012B/2493